Praise for *Anxiety*

"For decades, Art and Laraine Bennett have been laboring in the Lord's vineyard, helping countless men and women live with greater freedom and joy while following Christ ever more faithfully. Now they have teamed up with their daughter, Catholic psychologist Dr. Lianna Haidar, to address the crucial and timely topic of anxiety. With self-revealing honesty, candor, clinical experience, and spiritual wisdom, they gently bring our anxieties into the light and make them more understandable, more bearable, and much less frightening. As a result, this book will be a consolation and help to any anxious soul seeking the peace that passes all understanding (Phil. 4:7)."

—Andrew J. Sodergren, M.T.S., Psy.D., Director of
Psychological Services, Ruah Woods Psychological Services

"While all of us experience fear and anxiety at one time or another, the problem appears to be spiraling out of control in our 'advancing' modern society. Good Catholics and Christians, and even their ministers, are certainly not immune from this phenomenon. In this wonderful book, the Bennetts artfully and articulately balance science and faith in providing a guide to understand and address the problem. As a longtime and recovering worrywart, I highly recommend this book. Whether you or your loved ones have chronic struggles or just occasional bouts, there is much in this book that you will find helpful."

—Rev. Charles Sikorsky, L.C., J.D., J.C.L.,
President, Divine Mercy University

"Ours is indeed an age of anxiety. Students, colleagues, parents, everyone seems overbooked, overwhelmed, and 'stressed out,' either trying to avoid anxiety at all costs or else settling for a life that is fundamentally anxious. This new book tackles the question of anxiety: what is it, what happens when you avoid it, and what is the best way to address it to live a flourishing Christian life. Authors Art and Laraine Bennett team up with their psychologist daughter, Dr. Lianna Haidar, to tackle the besetting problem of our age."

—Andrew V. Abela, Ph.D., Dean, Busch School of Business;
Author, *Superhabits: The Universal System for a Successful Life*

"The Bennetts—with their daughter Dr. Haidar—take up a timely and timeless topic, artfully integrating psychology, biology, theology, philosophy, and literature in an engaging manner to shed light on the common experience of anxiety. With an accessible perspective and an authentically Catholic anthropology, this new book provides the reader with both an intellectual understanding and practical guidance on how staying 'in the boat' of Catholic teaching is a true asset for effective coping."

—*Frank J. Moncher, Ph.D.,* Licensed Clinical Psychologist

"In the crowded field of self-help books, *Anxiety* is a down-to-earth addition that can help us use the contributions of psychology to address the worries that impede joy and peace. The authors write in an honest and engaging style brimming with practical information, actionable advice, and perennial wisdom. This book shows what the lives and writings of the saints can tell us about how to address present-day anxieties. I would recommend this book to any Catholic with anxiety."

—*Dr. Eric M. Gudan, Psy.D., H.S.P.P.,* Licensed Clinical Psychologist, Integritas Psychological Services, Inc.

"In this book, the Bennetts provide clear and practical guidelines for cultivating mental health in the context of a holistic understanding of the human person. I heartily recommend it to anyone challenged by anxiety and to anybody who knows someone who struggles with anxiety. The Bennetts offer hope—anxiety is not a problem without a solution."

—*Rev. Donald J. Planty Jr., J.C.D.,* Pastor, St. Charles Borromeo Catholic Church, Arlington, Virginia

"In response to the rise of anxiety in our modern world, the Bennetts have provided us with a wonderful resource that blends neuroscience, psychology, and the fullness of the Catholic Faith. Drawing on insights from leading researchers and stories from the saints, this book helps us develop an understanding of anxiety and how we can respond in order to live more peaceful lives, free of worry and fear."

—*Ian Masson, L.P.C.,* Owner, Agape Counseling and Consulting

"When anxiety wants to take over, when rest and sleep are elusive, *Anxiety: A Catholic Guide to Freedom from Worry and Fear* will lift the burdens and help you go into the future in a wholesome way. The authors integrate Scripture, the saints, clinical expertise, and spiritual insights. The personal anecdotes provide wisdom and hope. The mystery of the human person is unpacked and wrapped in God's love, a love for you that's better than you think. I want to have this book close by in my pastoral ministry."

—***Rev. Msgr. Bob Cilinski,*** Episcopal Vicar for Charitable Works, Diocese of Arlington; Pastor, Nativity Catholic Church

Anxiety

ART A. BENNETT, L.M.F.T., LARAINE BENNETT, M.A.,
AND LIANNA BENNETT HAIDAR, PSY.D.

Anxiety

A Catholic Guide to Freedom from Worry and Fear

SOPHIA INSTITUTE PRESS
Manchester, New Hampshire

Sophia Institute Press
Box 5284, Manchester, NH 03108
1-800-888-9344
www.SophiaInstitute.com

Sophia Institute Press® is a registered trademark of Sophia Institute.

paperback ISBN 979-8-88911-106-1

ebook ISBN 979-8-88911-107-8

Library of Congress Control Number: 2025932929

First printing

To our families

Contents

PART ONE
What Is Anxiety

PART TWO
Unhelpful Strategies

PART THREE
Leaning into Anxiety

Acknowledgments

WE ARE GRATEFUL for the pioneering leadership of Charlie McKinney, and for our publicity queen Sarah Lemieux, editors Anna Maria Dube and Ellen Toner, marketing manager Molly Rublee, and everyone else at Sophia Institute Press who believed in this project and helps bring our books to life. We also want to acknowledge our clients, who place their trust in us, and for whom we hope this book might be an additional aid to growth. We are also immensely grateful to our families, especially Steve, Elias, and Taya, who put up with long hours spent discussing, debating, typing feverishly, and ordering DoorDash dinners while occasional chaos ensued.

Authors' Note

Litany of Consolation
by Fr. Peter John Cameron, O.P.[1]

When the darkness of depression overshadows me — Lord Jesus, You say: *I am the Light of the world.*

When plagued by my fragility and all my limitations — Lord Jesus, You say: *Blessed are the poor in spirit; the kingdom of God is theirs.*

When sadness takes hold of me — Lord Jesus, You say: *Blessed are the sorrowing; they shall be consoled.*

When tormented by my insecurity and my inadequacy — Lord Jesus, You say: *Blessed are the lowly; they shall inherit the earth.*

When lost and unsure about where to turn — Lord Jesus, You say: *Your Father knows what you need before you ask Him.*

When fretful and obsessive about so many things — Lord Jesus, You say: *Do not worry about what you are to eat or drink or use for clothing.*

---

[1] Reprinted with permission from Magnificat, LLC (Yonkers, NY: Magnificat.com, 2024), www.magnificat.com.

When lethargy and listlessness take over—Lord Jesus, You say: *Seek first the Father's kingship over you and all will be given you.*

When worry about the future paralyzes me—Lord Jesus, You say: *Let tomorrow take care of itself.*

When I feel helpless and forsaken—Lord Jesus, You say: *Ask and you will receive.*

When shame and guilt overwhelm me—Lord Jesus, You say: *I have come to call not the self-righteous, but sinners.*

When engulfed by anxiety and fear—Lord Jesus, You say: *Do not be afraid of anything.*

When my life lacks any purpose or direction—Lord Jesus, You say: *Follow me.*

When I believe I am worthless and a total disappointment—Lord Jesus, You say: *You are worth more than an entire flock of sparrows.*

When weighed down by the addictions of my life—Lord Jesus, You say: *Come to me all you who are weary and find life burdensome.*

When the harshness and ruthlessness of life assail me—Lord Jesus, You say: *I am gentle and humble of heart; your souls will find rest.*

When it seems I have only a little to offer—Lord Jesus, You say: *To the one who has, more will be given.*

When I crave approval and fear the judgment of others—Lord Jesus, You say: *Whoever becomes lowly like a little child is of greatest importance in the kingdom of God.*

When I'm feeling discouraged because of my body—Lord Jesus, You say: *Remain in me. Do not be afraid of anything.*

When my situation seems hopeless—Lord Jesus, You say: *For God, all things are possible.*

When I fear that my life is irrelevant and insignificant—Lord Jesus, You say: *The last shall be first.*

When I'm afraid to face the truth about myself—Lord Jesus, You say: *Whoever humbles himself shall be exalted.*

When exhausted by tedium, tiresomeness, and stress—Lord Jesus, You say*: Come by yourselves to an out-of-the-way place and rest a little.*

When terrified by the raging storms of life—Lord Jesus, You say: *Do not be afraid; it is I.*

When I am full of doubt, with no one to depend on—Lord Jesus, You say: *Everything is possible to one who trusts.*

When it's hard to persevere and I'm tempted to give up—Lord Jesus, You say: *By patient endurance you will save your lives.*

When bitterness and resentment poison my heart—Lord Jesus, You say: *If the Son frees you, you will be truly free.*

When I feel like I belong to no one—Lord Jesus, You say: *I know my sheep and my sheep know me.*

When I see nothing but my wrongdoing and failures—Lord Jesus, You say: *Do not let your heart be troubled; have faith in me.*

When swayed by moralism, relativism, and nihilism—Lord Jesus, You say: *I am the way, the truth, and the life.*

When I'm feeling cut off, alienated, and alone—Lord Jesus, You say: *I am the vine, you are the branches.*

When duped by self-absorption and self-obsessiveness—Lord Jesus, You say: *Apart from me you can do nothing.*

When despairing because of isolation and alienation—Lord Jesus, You say: *I will not leave you orphans.*

When downcast from feeling friendless and betrayed—Lord Jesus, You say: *I call you friends.*

When I refuse to believe that anyone could love me—Lord Jesus, You say: *It was not you who chose me; it was I who chose you.*

When tempted to apathy, cynicism, and dread—Lord Jesus, You say: *Ask and you shall receive, that your joy may be full.*

When polluted by the hatred and violence of the world—Lord Jesus, You say: *Take courage; I have overcome the world.*

When I think that happiness is nothing but a delusion—Lord Jesus, You ask me: *Do you love me?*

When my life reaches a dead end and I lack all desire—Lord Jesus, You ask me: *Do you love me?*

When I decide that life has no meaning—Lord Jesus, You ask me: *Do you love me?*

Yes, Lord Jesus, I do!—Lord Jesus, You say: *Live on in my love.*

Anxiety

What Is Anxiety

CHAPTER 1

The Age of Anxiety

Then back they come,
The fears that we fear. We fall asleep
Only to meet the idiot children of
Our revels and wrongs; farouche they appear,
Reluctant look-behinds, loitering through
The mooing gate, menacing or smiling,
Nocturnal trivia, torts and dramas . . .
yet we shiver:
For athwart our thinking the threat looms.
—W. H. Auden[1]

"I feel as though my chest is being squeezed
by an iron fist and I struggle to catch a
breath. Along with the physical sensation,
I feel panicky and unfocused."

"I'm breathing rapidly, as though
I already sprinted a mile, and my
heart is pounding. My overwhelming
thought is of how badly everything

---

[1] W. H. Auden, *The Age of Anxiety: A Baroque Eclogue* (Princeton: Princeton University Press, 2011), 17.

*is going to turn out, all the negative
emotions, gloom and doom."*

*"I was jolted awake in the middle of
the night; my heart was pounding,
and I was gasping for air. I jumped
out of bed because I didn't know
what was happening to me!"*

*"It's everything; I worry about the
kids, what they eat, what I'll make for
dinner, how homework will get done,
the shopping, plans for tomorrow, next
week, next year—it all piles up and
I can barely focus on one worry when
another worry comes right on its heels."*

*"I feel my face flush, I start sweating,
and my mind goes blank."*

It's rare to find a person who hasn't had moments of intense anxiety like these, or who hasn't gone through phases of dread and worry. And everyone has experienced that twinge of anxiety, small or large, whether it comes after receiving a curt e-mail saying the boss wants to speak to you in an hour, or along with a panicky feeling as you wonder whether you'll be able to make the payments on that new loan you took out. And most of us are familiar with the anxiety that comes when facing particular types of situations—for example, when flying in an airplane, looking out from the top of a high building, giving a speech, or facing a large crowd of strangers. Others experience anxiety when recalling a past traumatic event. And some people suffer from constant worrying—ruminating over possible disasters or being unable to stop the negative what-if scenarios. Still others experience a generalized, paralyzing dread that permeates their daily lives, like a large black cloud hanging overhead, sapping their energy and focus.

Anxiety is commonly understood as a feeling of worry, nervousness, or unease, typically about a *future* threat; we can distinguish it from fear, which is the response to a real or perceived *imminent* threat.[2] We may have a feeling of dread upon awakening, or we feel constantly overwhelmed (as opposed to simply being busy). We may also feel as though we're in a state of threat, or our anxiety may manifest as constant brain fog, irritability, and fatigue.

For some, the anxiety permeates everything, impacting the quality of their daily lives and their relationships. *The Diagnostic and Statistical Manual of Mental Disorders, Fifth Edition, Text Revision* (DSM-5-TR), used by mental health clinicians, defines anxiety that has reached a level of clinical diagnosis—a level requiring intervention—as "excessive anxiety and worry (apprehensive expectation) occurring more days than not for at least 6 months." The DSM explains that individuals experiencing this state find it difficult to control the worry and the anxiety, which manifest themselves in three or more of the following presentations: restlessness, fatigue,

---

[2]   Though fear and anxiety states often overlap, they also differ, as noted in the *Diagnostic and Statistical Manual of Mental Disorders, 5th Edition, Text Revision* (Washington, DC: American Psychiatric Association, 2022), 215.

difficulty of concentration, irritability, and muscle tension.[3] Anxiety may be generalized, or it may relate to specific objects or situations, but anxiety disorders differ from a passing incidence of anxiety by being persistent (the guideline is lasting longer than six months).[4]

When anxiety has such an outsize impact on someone's life, it reaches a clinically diagnosable level. But what is the dividing line, the threshold, for diagnosis? It's essentially the difference between experiencing an occasional headache versus having a pattern of chronic headaches that warrant a talk with your primary care doctor. You also might think of it as the difference between having an occasional argument with your spouse that is quickly resolved versus fighting every day with your spouse without resolution. A slightly finer analogy would be the difference between being tired after a week of intense work versus feeling chronically burned out.

ANXIETY TODAY

Anxiety is increasing in our modern world—in fact, anxiety disorders are the most commonly diagnosed of all mental disorders.[5] In the early 2000s, the National Institute of Mental Health estimated that about 31 percent of adults in the United

---

[3] Ibid., 250.

[4] Ibid., 215.

[5] Christopher Palmer, *Brain Energy: A Revolutionary Breakthrough in Understanding Mental Health—and Improving Treatment for Anxiety, Depression, OCD, PTSD, and More* (Dallas: BenBella Books, 2022), 12.

States would experience an anxiety disorder in their lives.[6] By 2018, 39 percent of Americans reported being more anxious than they were the prior year, and another 39 percent had the same level of anxiety as the prior year. "That's nearly 80 percent of the population" experiencing anxiety.[7]

And this was all pre-COVID.

A systematic review of data published in *The Lancet* shows that anxiety and depression increased globally due to COVID-19.[8] And, in fact, the rates of *all* mental health disorders are rising today—and not simply because we are more aware of them.[9] Awareness of anxiety is certainly greater today than in previous generations, thanks in large part to the rise of social media. But social media is a double-edged sword: It also gives rise to anxiety![10]

One might think that, globally, people in countries plagued by war, terrorism, persecutions, disease, and food and water shortages might be more anxious than those of us who live in first-world countries, but this is not always the case; the prevalence of anxiety disorders is actually highest

---

[6] Judson Brewer, *Unwinding Anxiety: New Science Shows How to Break the Cycles of Worry and Fear to Heal Your Mind* (New York: Avery, 2021), 12.

[7] Ibid.

[8] Damian Santomauro et al., "Global Prevalence and Burden of Depressive and Anxiety Disorders in 204 Countries and Territories in 2020 due to the COVID-19 Pandemic," *Lancet* 398, no. 10312 (Nov. 6, 2021): 1700–1712, https://doi.org/10.1016/S0140-6736(21)02143-7.

[9] Palmer, *Brain Energy*, 16.

[10] Anna Vannucci et al., "Social Media Use and Anxiety in Emerging Adults," *Journal of Affective Disorders* 207 (2017): 163–166, https://doi.org/10.1016/j.jad.2016.08.040.

in high-income countries.[11] As Dr. Anna Lembke writes in her best-selling book *Dopamine Nation*, "Over the past three decades, I have seen growing numbers of patients … who appear to have every advantage in life — supportive families, quality education, financial stability, good health — yet [they] develop debilitating anxiety, depression, and physical pain."[12]

Anxiety today is common in many different diagnoses, both psychiatric and medical. You might see this distinction play out in someone who thinks, "Well, if I just had a heart attack, of course I'd be anxious!" In such a scenario, the anxiety would likely have started as a psychiatric issue but grown into a medical one; it may be that anxiety plays a role in contributing to cardiovascular disease, as well as to other diseases. While we have established that the overall prevalence of anxiety in the general population is very high on a regular basis, even more alarming is that "when looking at lifetime prevalence," the percent of people who will experience an anxiety disorder "rises to 33 percent, meaning that one out of three people will meet the criteria for an anxiety disorder at some point in their life."[13]

Internationally acclaimed contemporary philosopher Byung-Chul Han comments that every age has its signature afflictions. Our age doesn't suffer so much from an excess of negativity as, for example, the previous generation did when fighting the Cold War (one might argue that everyone was

---

[11] Brewer, *Unwinding Anxiety*, 13.

[12] Anna Lembke, *Dopamine Nation: Finding Balance in the Age of Indulgence* (New York: Dutton, 2021), 37.

[13] Palmer, *Brain Energy*, 57.

engaged in an us-versus-them mindset in that climate). Today, we suffer from the opposite problem: an excess of *positivity*. What do we mean by this? When anything is said to be possible, from the option to have whatever career one wants to the possibility of changing one's own gender, where nothing is impossible—and when we are answerable to no one—the result is "hectic nervousness" and depression.[14]

In short, our age is one of anxiety.

UNDERSTANDING ANXIETY THROUGH SCRIPTURE

In startling contrast to the general mindset of anxiety that we confront each day, either personally or in the lives of the people around us, Jesus tells us, "Therefore do not be anxious about tomorrow, for tomorrow will be anxious for itself. Let the day's own trouble be sufficient for the day" (Matt. 6:34). And again, "As for the seed that fell among thorns, they are the ones who have heard [the word of God], but as they go along, they are choked by the anxieties … of life, and they fail to produce mature fruit" (Luke 8:14, NABRE).

And St. Paul writes to the Philippians, "Have no anxiety at all, but in everything by prayer and supplication with thanksgiving let your requests be made known to God. And the peace of God, which passes all understanding, will keep your hearts and your minds in Christ Jesus" (Phil. 4:6–7).

So how should we respond to the overriding malady of our day? *Have no anxiety at all.*

---

[14] See Byung-Chul Han, *The Burnout Society* (Stanford: Stanford University Press, 2015), 1–3, 11–18.

Does it mean that I am not a good Christian if I suffer from anxiety? Not at all! We can look to even more ancient Scripture for a meditation on this point.

Sacred Scripture records for us the moving words of Jeremiah the prophet, an Old Testament figure who was a type of Christ. After having prophesied for God, Jeremiah was beaten and thrown into the stocks by Pashhur, a priest of the Lord (Jer. 20:1). Jeremiah was greatly distressed by the way he was treated, and he cried out to God, "I have become a laughingstock all the day; every one mocks me" (20:7). In anguish he cried, "Terror is on every side! 'Denounce him! Let us denounce him!' say all my familiar friends, watching for my fall" (20:10).

And King David, another type of Christ, wrote movingly about the treachery of a friend, which is likened to the betrayal of Jesus by Judas: "My heart is in anguish within me, the terrors of death have fallen upon me. Fear and trembling come upon me, and horror overwhelms me" (Ps. 55:4–5).

The book of Sirach, the last of the Wisdom books in the Catholic canon of the Old Testament, contains a reflection on anxiety as part of the condition of man, whether one "sits on a splendid throne" or "is humbled in dust and ashes":

> Their perplexities and fear of heart — their anxious thought is the day of death, from the man who sits on a splendid throne to the one who is humbled in dust and ashes, from the man who wears purple and a crown to the one who is clothed in burlap; there is anger and envy and trouble and unrest, and fear of death, and fury

and strife. And when one rests upon his bed, his sleep at night confuses his mind. He gets little or no rest, and afterward in his sleep, as though he were on watch, he is troubled by the visions of his mind like one who has escaped from the battle-front; at the moment of his rescue he wakes up, and wonders that his fear came to nothing. (Sir. 40:2–7)

ANXIETY IN THE LIVES OF THE SAINTS

Even saints suffered from anxiety. Saints suffered physical ailments, as all ordinary humans do. And so, too, many saints suffered from mental anguish, including depression and anxiety. They are saints because they practiced heroic virtue, not because they are inhuman or have no defects or struggles in life.

Thérèse of Lisieux, saint and Doctor of the Church—the beloved Little Flower—had a very difficult period in her youth when she struggled with what we might now call depression and anxiety. Reflecting on the effect that the tragedy of her mother's death had on her when she was just four years old, she later wrote that "my happy disposition completely changed after Mama's death. I, once so full of life, became timid and retiring, sensitive to an excessive degree."[15] Her father, her dear Papa, moved their family to Les Buissonnets in Lisieux after the loss of his wife so that his daughters could be closer to their cousins. Thérèse had many happy times in their

---

[15] Thérèse of Lisieux, *Story of a Soul Study Edition*, trans. John Clarke, O.C.D. (Washington, DC: ICS Publications, 2019), 49.

new home with him, taking nature walks, cultivating flowers in her own little garden, and playing board games and other imaginative games with her sisters and cousins. It was during this time that her second oldest sister, Pauline, became a second mother to her. However, when Thérèse was sent to boarding school at the age of eight, her secure and self-contained world was challenged. Having never been away from her close-knit family, and also not having had any experience of playing with other children outside of that family circle, she didn't know how to make friends with the other schoolgirls. Furthermore, as she was the youngest in her class and yet the most intelligent and well loved by all the teachers, the other girls began to shun her and were quite cruel; this led to Thérèse spending time alone while at school, "sad and sick," as she put it.[16] She didn't even share these sufferings with her sisters. This must have been a rather traumatic experience for the extremely sensitive (and somewhat cosseted) Thérèse, who was additionally suffering from the anxiety of scrupulosity—until her father removed her from the school after five long years. Thérèse later wrote, "The five years I spent in school were the saddest in my life."[17]

It was during her second year at school that her beloved Pauline left, to become a cloistered nun at Carmel; a few months after Pauline's departure, a mysterious illness overtook Thérèse. She later described it as if she were being attacked by a demon. She suffered hallucinations and nervous trembling. In fact, it was likely the combined and compounded result of the anxiety of her school environment added to the trauma

16 Ibid., 132.
17 Ibid., 81.

from her mother's death being relived when Pauline, her "second mother," left for Carmel: "I didn't understand and I said in the depths of my heart, 'Pauline is lost to me!'"[18]

At the young age of nine she had lost two mothers! She wrote that it "broke [her] heart when Jesus took away her dear Mama, her tenderly loved Pauline!"[19] For Thérèse, the deprivation of her sister felt as if Pauline was lost to her "almost in the same manner as if she were dead."[20]

She began experiencing constant headaches and then, being very fatigued while she was home from school during Easter vacation, she suddenly began trembling and was plunged into a terrible illness, which she herself believed came from a demon. "I can't describe this strange sickness, but I'm now convinced it was the work of the devil," Thérèse would write more than a decade later, in 1895.[21] From October to March, when Pauline was in Carmel and receiving formation in preparation for taking the habit (a ceremony Thérèse wanted to attend), Thérèse experienced headaches, fatigue, shivering, and weeping. After the ceremony itself, during which Thérèse was perfectly fine and able to be in attendance, her disease entered a new, violent stage.[22] From the middle of March to the tenth of May, long comas alternated with fits of violent shrieking and agitation, and Thérèse would cry out that she saw frightening things—even one time screaming that her beloved Papa was a horrible black animal, which

---

18   Ibid., 90.
19   Ibid., 87.
20   Ibid., 133.
21   Ibid., 92.
22   Ida Friederike Görres, *The Hidden Face* (San Francisco: Ignatius Press, 2003), 78–79.

caused him to flee, weeping, from the room. St. Thérèse said that her eventual cure came through the Blessed Mother: "A miracle was necessary and it was our Lady of Victories who worked it."[23]

Her physician, Dr. Notta, classed her illness as St. Vitus's Dance, also known as chorea. But French Dominican R. P. H. Petitot, in his biography, attributed the illness to "psychic tension."[24] "All witnesses agree that the illness represented an eruption of overwhelming anxiety fantasies."[25]

In the nineteenth century, especially in a devoutly religious family, the notion of trauma leading to a serious anxiety disorder was not available. But in reality, grief piles on grief, and trauma on trauma. We have a much better understanding and appreciation today for the fact that any new loss can open up all past grief wounds, sometimes as if they had never healed. Such things as feeling out of control in her own body, shutting down into a comatose state, and experiencing nightmares are all anxiety and trauma symptoms that fit the picture of a young child who has lost her mother, and then her sister, and is socially alienated and rejected by her peers.

St. Jane Frances de Chantal also suffered from anxiety. She was the wife of the Baron de Chantal, with whom she had six children. But in 1601, when she was only twenty-eight, her beloved husband was killed in a hunting accident; she

---

[23] Thérèse, *Story of a Soul*, 95.

[24] Görres, *The Hidden Face*, 81. Görres here refers to *Vie Intégrale de Sainte Thérèse* by R. P. H. Petitot, O.P., written in 1925.

[25] Ibid., 82.

then raised her four living children as a single mother while also taking on the management of the family estate. St. Francis de Sales, who was one of her contemporaries, became her friend and spiritual director just a few years later, in 1603. In 1610, with his guidance, she founded the Visitation Sisters of Mary, a religious order that served the poor and sick. Perhaps St. Francis de Sales had in mind Jane's struggle with anxiety when he wrote, "Anxiety is the greatest evil which can happen to the soul, sin only excepted."[26]

Though Jane was a remarkably strong and successful woman, throughout her life she suffered from depression and anxiety: "A few months after I became a widow ... it pleased God that my whole being should be beset by so many different, distressing temptations that, if he in his mercy had not taken pity on me, I am sure I should have perished in the fury of that storm, for I could get almost no relief from this anxiety, and I lost so much weight that I became quite unlike myself—you would hardly have recognized me."[27] And again, in a letter to St. Francis de Sales, she wrote, "Death itself, it seems to me, would be less painful to bear than the distress of mind which this occasions, and I feel as if all things had power to harm me. I am afraid of everything; I live in dread."[28]

---

[26] Francis de Sales, *Introduction to the Devout Life* (London: Rivington, 1876; Veritatis Splendor Publications, 2012), 199.

[27] Bert Ghezzi, *Saints at Heart: How Fault-Filled, Problem-Prone, Imperfect People like Us Can Be Holy* (Brewster, MA: Paraclete Press, 2019), 134.

[28] Jane Frances de Chantal, *Selected Letters of St. Jane Frances de Chantal,* trans. the Sisters of the Visitation (London: Washbourne, 1918; Project Gutenberg, 2015), 10, https://www.gutenberg.org/files/50592/50592-h/50592-h.htm.

These two saints and many others have experienced the depths of sadness, fatigue, and anxiety, yet they never ceased loving God and serving others heroically—and often those closest to them were not even aware of their intense suffering.

APPLYING A CHRISTIAN LENS TO AN ANCIENT MALADY

"Have no anxiety about anything" (Phil. 4:6). If even the saints struggled with it, what are we to do? None of us consciously seeks out more anxiety and stress. Surely none of us go to bed at night saying, "I really need to worry more!" And neither do we go to our doctor asking for a medication that will *increase* our anxiety. On the contrary, rationally and with a Christian lens, we approach the subject of anxiety, seeking relief, both emotionally and spiritually. We want—that is, we lack and are looking to find—a way to get from this place of anxiety, worry, and distress, where the saints have suffered along with the rest of us, to that place in which Scripture promises us that we will receive that peace of God that surpasses all understanding. In every Mass during the Communion Rite, after the Lord's Prayer, we pray, asking God that "by the help of your mercy, we may be always free from sin and *safe from all distress*, as we await the blessed hope and the coming of our Savior, Jesus Christ" (emphasis added). That's what we want. That's the goal.

And indeed, it is possible and even necessary to not let anxiety control our lives, not only for our own sake but for the sake of our family, friends, and co-workers. But there is no quick fix to this, no matter how well we know and appreciate what the goal is, and what the saints and Scripture have timelessly mapped out for us in past centuries and millennia. A problem that has been prevalent in the human experience since the earliest recorded histories cannot have a simple solution.

In truth, the concept of anxiety goes all the way back to Hippocrates and the ancient Greeks. They understood anxiety (i.e., the state of anxiety, as opposed to a tendency to be anxious) as a medical condition—one that affected both the mind and the body, in contrast with other maladies of negative affect: "Anxiety was clearly identified as a distinct negative affect and as a separate disorder by Greco-Roman philosophers and physicians. In addition, ancient philosophy suggested treatments for anxiety that are not too far removed from today's cognitive approaches."[29] One source tells us how Hippocrates specifically describes the terrors of a man named Nicanor, who was filled with "fear of the flute girl" at evening drinking parties; whenever he heard her begin to play, "masses of terrors rose up."[30]

This same source also provides a brief etymology of the word *anxiety*, highlighting its ancient roots: "[It] derives from the Latin substantive *angor* and the corresponding verb *ango* (to constrict). A cognate word is *angustus* (narrow). These words derive from an Indo-European root that has produced *Angst* in modern German (and related words in Dutch, Danish, Norwegian, and Swedish). Interestingly, the same relationship between the idea of narrowness and anxiety is

---

[29] Marc-Antoine Crocq, "A History of Anxiety: From Hippocrates to DSM," *Dialogues in Clinical Neuroscience* 17, no. 3 (2015): 319–325, https://doi.org/10.31887/DCNS.2015.17.3/macrocq.

[30] Ibid. (directly quoting Hippocrates in *Epidemics*).

attested in Biblical Hebrew. In fact, Job expresses his anguish (Job 7:10) literally with the Hebrew expression 'the *narrowness* (*tsar*) of my spirit.'"[31]

Confronting Anxiety Today

Shifting our focus back from the saints and the ancients, consider how what they experienced, witnessed, and described is evident in our world today.

Are you, as we discussed earlier, feeling *constantly* overwhelmed, as opposed to simply being busy or having a stressful week or two at work? Are you continually experiencing that fight-flight-freeze response, or struggling with that constant brain fog and irritability? Dr. Sara Gottfried writes, "Consistent across all feelings that fall under the heading of anxiety is an overreactive set of thoughts, a mind that cultivates counterproductive responses to a situation. The thoughts are felt emotionally (dread, overwhelm, panic, etc.) *and* physically (breathlessness, heart racing, sweating, chest pain or discomfort, etc.).... Evolution has primed us to be this way—and it takes a new level of awareness and discernment to bring the brain and body back into balance."[32] We will get into the details of what various counterproductive responses to anxiety look like in later chapters, but the key takeaway to focus on in these words from Gottfried is that many times our initial tendency to react a certain way to dispel the anxiety ultimately can create *more* anxiety.

[31] Ibid.
[32] Sara Gottfried, *Brain Body Diet: 40 Days to a Lean, Calm, Energized, and Happy Self* (New York: HarperOne, 2019), 225.

Simply put, all too often, our attempted solution to anxiety actually makes the problem worse!

Most of us have experienced periodic episodes of anxiety, so we're familiar with Gottfried's descriptions of some of its various manifestations. But, as we mentioned earlier, chronic anxiety is on the rise, meaning that many of us today are experiencing anxiety even more frequently than just in mere episodic instances, even if we're not formally diagnosed with anxiety disorder. What that means, unfortunately, is that, for many of us, what once was abnormal anxiety is now becoming the new normal. As therapists, we have noticed when we see new clients that anxiety often walks in the room first and takes a seat—even before the new client does.

Even more concerning is that anxiety is on the rise in children.[33] When we consider that anxiety may be a "gateway" to other conditions—such as depression, addiction, and even suicide[34]—its effect on our children becomes that much more troubling. As many researchers have pointed out, anxiety symptoms are *bidirectional*—that is, they both cause other medical or psychiatric conditions and are caused by them.

Ours is an anxious age, with anxiety abounding in the headlines, in our churches, our neighborhoods and schools, our communities, our politics, and even in our immediate homes and families. What can we do to confront it? Fundamentally, there are three options:

---

[33] Wolters Kluwer Health, "More Than 1 in 20 U.S. Children and Teens Have Anxiety or Depression," ScienceDaily, April 24, 2018, www.sciencedaily.com/releases/2018/04/180424184119.htm.
[34] Gottfried, *Brain Body Diet*, 228.

1. We can live in fear about the fear. We can obsess about the anxiety, become more anxious about being anxious, and ultimately cause it to spread and multiply in such a way that it becomes unmanageable.

2. We can avoid the anxiety and attempt to avoid anything or anyone who makes us feel anxious. We create rigid, impermeable boundaries around ourselves and eliminate anything that might make us anxious, nervous, or upset. This response isolates, disconnects, and withdraws—and our world becomes smaller and smaller.

3. This book is about the third option. We face our anxiety head-on. We assess the problem calmly and rationally, while remaining connected to others and to ourselves and working to address the anxiety itself.

How do we do this? Well, we've started already, simply by getting a better understanding of what anxiety is, how it affects us, how it has affected all people from the earliest days to today, and how the saints and individuals in Scripture have suffered from it and confronted it. Our next step will be to look more closely at three things: the connection between fear and anxiety, contemporary neuroscience, and the curious case of the woman with no amygdala.

Chapter 2

The Brain and Anxiety

All that exists
Matters to man; he minds what happens
And feels he is at fault, a fallen soul
With power to place, to explain every
What in the world but why he is neither
God nor good, this guilt the insoluble
Final fact, infusing his private
Nexus of needs, his noted aims with
Incomprehensible comprehensive dread.

—W. H. Auden[35]

SURVIVAL FUELED BY FEAR

Known to the world only by her initials, S. M. has a rare condition called Urbach-Wiethe disease that completely destroyed part of her brain: the amygdala. Because of this rare condition and the resulting "neuropsychological profile remarkable for a history of defective personal and social

---

[35] W. H. Auden, *The Age of Anxiety: A Baroque Eclogue* (Princeton: Princeton University Press, 2011), 20.

decision-making,"[36] she has been studied by researchers for many years. To put it succinctly, S. M. experiences no fear. In interviews, she said that she doesn't know how to judge whether an individual is trustworthy, and she shared that she has readily engaged with people quite indiscriminately. She has been attacked several times and even held at knifepoint. On one occasion, after successfully fending off an attacker, she then asked him for a ride. Snakes and tarantulas don't faze her; when shown the scariest of horror movies, she'll ask for the names so she can rent them later; and she can walk through a terrifying haunted house with only curiosity, even when a "monster" jumps out at her.

Alex Honnold is a world-famous free-solo rock climber who is the subject of the riveting (and terrifying even to watch!) National Geographic documentary *Free Solo*, in which he climbs the three-thousand-foot El Capitan in Yosemite National Park. He does this alone, with no ropes nor any protection of any kind. As you're watching it, you realize that if he falls, he dies. Despite all that, however, Honnold said in an interview, "I certainly don't think of myself as a big risk taker."[37] As it turns out, doctors discovered in the course of conducting some brain imaging on him that his brain has below-normal amygdala activation.[38]

---

[36] R. Adolphs et al., "Impaired Recognition of Emotion in Facial Expressions following Bilateral Damage to the Human Amygdala," *Nature* 372 (1994): 669–672, https://doi.org/10.1038/372669a0.

[37] Owen Clark, "Alex Honnold, Free Soloist, Star of Academy-Award-Winning Documentary Free Solo," *Climbing*, last updated May 3, 2022, https://www.climbing.com/people/alex-honnold-rock-climber-academy-award-winning-documentary-free-solo/.

[38] Anna Lembke, *Dopamine Nation: Finding Balance in the Age of Indulgence* (New York: Dutton, 2021), 158.

The amygdala (a pair of almond-shaped structures inside the temporal lobe) is the part of our brain that controls fear. As Dr. Bessel van der Kolk puts it, the amygdala is the "smoke detector of the brain." Its job is to identify threats to our survival.[39]

From at least the time of our cave-dwelling ancestors facing saber-toothed tigers and woolly mammoths, the brain has had to develop survival mechanisms to face daily life-threatening situations. The "smoke detector" has to work extremely fast. In fact, it will bypass our rational brain to send signals to the body to fight or run away—or in common terminology, to engage basic survival responses of fight, flight, or freeze—even without our conscious awareness.

A helpful analogy for understanding the human brain is to think of it having an upstairs and a downstairs, like in a house. The downstairs is the oldest part of the brain, controlling innate reactions, such as fight-flight-freeze, and strong emotions, such as anger and fear—all of which are necessary to survival. The upstairs brain is more sophisticated and evolved, where rational mental processes such as thinking, planning, and managing our emotions take place.[40] The amygdala, of course, is located in our "downstairs" brain; it sets in motion the bodily reactions necessary to survival. "The amygdala's danger signals trigger the release of powerful stress hormones, including cortisol and adrenaline, which increase heart rate, blood pressure,

---

[39] Bessel van der Kolk, *The Body Keeps the Score: Brain, Mind, and Body in the Healing of Trauma* (New York: Penguin Books, 2014), 56, 60.

[40] Daniel Siegel and Tina Payne Bryson, *The Whole-Brain Child: 12 Revolutionary Strategies to Nurture Your Child's Developing Mind* (New York: Bantam Books, 2012), 38ff.

and rate of breathing, preparing us to fight back or run away."[41] The threat information is processed so quickly that, even before we're consciously aware of danger—say, a speeding car heading for us—we are already jumping out of the way. In such situations, the brain has already sent signals to all the parts of the body involved in facing or escaping the threat: Muscles in the chest and stomach tighten, breathing quickens, and the heart beats faster. This auto-response is lifesaving when there is an immediate threat and we don't have time to think things through. Fear is an emotion vital to our survival. In fact, those ancestors who were fearless—or those who wanted to think things through more carefully—may not have survived the attack of the saber-toothed tiger.

FEAR AND ANXIETY

So how does fear relate to anxiety? Doctors of antiquity (recall Hippocrates and the "fear of the flute player" from chapter 1) and medieval theologians (notably St. Thomas Aquinas) have puzzled over the exact relationship between fear and anxiety. Even today, we are still puzzling over this.[42]

According to Aquinas, anxiety is a particular kind of fear—a fear that arises when we dread (or *imagine*) an external evil that is unforeseen. He distinguishes this type of fear (i.e., anxiety) from other types of fear. These different types of fear are related to the different sorts of evil being confronted:

---

[41] Van der Kolk, *Score*, 61.

[42] See, for example, "The Overlap between Fear and Anxiety Brain Circuits: Contrary to Previous Theories, Fear and Anxiety Reflect Shared Neural Building Blocks," ScienceDaily, September 21, 2020, www.sciencedaily.com/releases/2020/09/200921130629.htm.

On the other hand, the evil that consists in external things may surpass man's faculty of resistance in three ways. First by reason of its magnitude; when, that is to say, a man considers some great evil the outcome of which he is unable to gauge: and then there is "amazement." Secondly, by reason of its being unwonted; because, to wit, some unwonted evil arises before us, and on that account is great in our estimation: and then there is "stupor," which is caused by the representation of something unwonted. *Thirdly, by reason of its being unforeseen: thus future misfortunes are feared, and fear of this kind is called "anxiety."*[43]

We can intuitively understand the first sort of fear that Aquinas describes; this is something that surpasses what we can actually comprehend in terms of magnitude, and can be an awe-inspiring fear, such as when we're in the path of a tsunami or experiencing a massive earthquake. The second fear he describes is the one that arises in the face of an evil so great that we have no fight-or-flight response. Instead, we simply freeze or give up, such as might happen when we are being held up at gunpoint. The third type of fear is the one that is really relevant to our discussion of anxiety, though it is helpful to understand the first two types of fear to know what anxiety is not. This third type of fear develops on account of things that are as yet "unforeseen" — that is, it is fear of things that are in the future. It

---

[43] Thomas Aquinas, *Summa Theologica* I-II, q. 41, art. 4, obj. 5, emphasis added.

is a fear of what *might happen*, of what we *imagine* could happen. In the first two examples (a tsunami bearing down on our beach house or being held up at gunpoint), it is entirely appropriate to react with our fight-flight-freeze response to an existing, present threat. Our amygdala was made for this!

Fear, according to the *Catechism of the Catholic Church* (*CCC*), is one of the passions. As such, it is never in itself sinful. Rather, our emotions are part of our human nature and are designed, in the case of fear, to alert us to evil or, in the case of love, to draw us to the good: "By his emotions man intuits the good and suspects evil" (*CCC*, 1771). It speaks earlier on this same idea when it instructs us that "the apprehension of evil causes hatred, aversion, and fear of the impending evil" (*CCC*, 1765).

Contemporary neuroscientists echo what Aquinas wrote when they say that anxiety is about the future; fear more generally, however, is understood to be about something immediately present, while trauma is about something from the past. To understand the distinctions among the three in practice, look at it this way. If you are *imagining* snakes being on the path you are walking, you may have *anxiety* about this possibility. If you actually *see* a rattlesnake in front of you, you will experience *fear*. If you have a visceral response to the memory of being bitten by a rattlesnake, this is *trauma*. While acknowledging that fear and anxiety overlap in many ways, the DSM-5-TR puts it this way: "*Fear* is the emotional response to real or perceived imminent threat, whereas *anxiety* is anticipation of future threat."[44]

---

[44] American Psychiatric Association, *Diagnostic and Statistical Manual of Mental Disorders, 5th Edition, Text Revision* (Washington, DC: American Psychiatric Association, 2022), 215.

One of Art's clients, Naomi,[45] was experiencing anxiety on a daily basis after taking on a new job. In her previous position, Naomi had been a top performer, but she had reached such a level of competence that the job no longer held sufficient challenges, so she took a promotion at a new company. Now each day was bringing unforeseen challenges and uncertainty: new boss, new job description, new crises every day. Each night, a stream of potential work disasters and worst-case scenarios ran through her mind, and she could not turn it off. Not being able to sleep caused more anxiety; lack of sleep then created a heightened sense of stress. It should come as no surprise that the sleep deprivation and the growing anxiety led to a classic downward spiral, feeding off each other. Constantly on edge, with an ever-growing sense of anxiety, Naomi began to feel as though she were in a constant state of threat.

When we apply the smoke-alarm analogy of the amygdala alerting us to a possible threat, and readying our body to the fight, flight, or freeze responses, we can see that quick action is vitally important if the threat is real and likely to endanger us (as in the flames are visible, and the smoke is entering the room). But whether life-threatening or not, we don't want our rational brain hijacked. We would rather have the opportunity to assess the situation. When Naomi heard the "fire alarm" in the middle of the night, she figuratively and immediately jumped out the window. Instead of first assessing the threat level, she immediately initiated maximum readiness of

---

[45] As explained in our Authors' Note, all names of clients in these pages are fictitious, and all situations and identifying features have been changed to preserve confidentiality. The stories are true, but many are an amalgamation of several clients in order to represent universal situations and preserve confidentiality.

DEFCON 1. It's possible that the fire alarm was simply a test. Or there was a malfunctioning battery. The worst-case scenario (a raging fire warranting immediate flight) was not actually the case. A hyperactive amygdala is like our brain hearing the fire alarm and, rather than assessing the situation as a possible threat that needs responding to—i.e., getting out of the building in a calm but prompt manner—the brain immediately screams, "Jump out the window *now!*"

With this analogy in mind, it's easy to understand why psychiatrist and neuroscientist Dr. Judson Brewer highlights that, whereas fear is adaptive and necessary to our survival, anxiety is a *maladaptive* response.[46] It's an indication of an impaired or over-activated stress response. You feel the stress response even when there's no serious or immediate threat. Our ancestors (those who survived, that is) were the ones whose fear responses saved them from the attack of that saber-toothed tiger. But in the absence of the tiger—or a very real threat of any kind—it's simply not healthy to be experiencing threat mode constantly.

The prefrontal cortex, sometimes dubbed the "CEO of the brain," is part of our rational (upstairs) brain, and so it is slower to respond. The prefrontal cortex is able to think things through, consider different options, and make predictions based on past experience. Dr. Bessel van der Kolk describes the prefrontal cortex as the "watchtower" that uses past experience to judge whether the present situation is actually a threat to life or whether there is some other explanation.[47] For example,

---

[46] Judson Brewer, *Unwinding Anxiety: New Science Shows How to Break the Cycles of Worry and Fear to Heal Your Mind* (New York: Avery, 2021), 17.

[47] Van der Kolk, *Score*, 62ff.

when we see a tiger in the zoo, we're not alarmed and the threat response is not engaged, because our prefrontal cortex steps in to remind us that the animal is safely contained. Our brains are very skilled at learning, distinguishing, and identifying different situations that may or may not be actual threats. But our prefrontal cortex does require accurate information in order to make good decisions and predictions. When that information is lacking, our rational brain begins to worry—and it can sometimes jump to inappropriate solutions. We can understand this sort of situation arising if we think of fear and anxiety being tied together specifically through uncertainty, demonstrated by this formula:[48]

$$\text{fear} + \text{uncertainty} = \text{anxiety}$$

This is not unlike Aquinas's description of anxiety as being defined by fear of future, *unforeseen* misfortunes.

Dr. Judson Brewer puts it this way: "Your thinking/planning brain doesn't have an information switch such that when it runs low on information, it goes into sleep mode until more information is available. Quite the opposite. 'Go get me some information!' it screams."[49] In such a situation, when your brain is ruminating over uncertainties, fretting about various negative "what ifs" (like Naomi, who was worrying about annoying her new boss if she asked any questions, alienating her colleagues, failing miserably on the new projects, and ultimately getting fired), it can spin out of control, and that's when the amygdala sets off the smoke alarm. Your body goes

---

[48] Brewer, Unwinding Anxiety, 19.
[49] Ibid., 20.

into fight-flight-freeze, and you experience a surge of adrenaline and increased blood pressure—all this even though you're not in mortal danger. Far from it. You are actually just lying in your bed, trying to go to sleep.[50]

THE AMYGDALA AS A MUSCLE

Anyone who has ever experienced a toddler having a meltdown has seen what happens when the amygdala hijacks the rational brain. Laraine was once at Sunday Mass with one of her grandchildren (who was two at the time), sitting somewhere near the front with the hope that proximity to the "action" would be instructive and interesting to him. Unfortunately, it was too interesting, and the two-year-old made a sprint for the altar. When the old grandparent finally caught him and grabbed him to take him away, the toddler launched into a full-blown screaming and writhing meltdown. At this point, his rational brain had literally been shut down by the amygdala; stress hormones were flooding his body, making it impossible for any number of logical or calming words to take effect.[51] The only solution was to make the long "walk

---

[50] The effect is *bidirectional*: anxiety interferes with sleep, and chronic sleep deprivation can cause anxiety disorders.

[51] The challenge for the parent is to find a way to calm the amygdala, realizing that words are not always likely to be effective. (That's why parents saying, "Stop this tantrum *right now* or you will be in even more trouble," tends not to work if the source of the tantrum is the amygdala. It may result in freeze behavior, which could temporarily appear to work but actually doesn't teach the child emotional regulation.) There are ways to calm the amygdala (moving to a different spot, rubbing their back comfortingly, dancing, listening to music, using soothing tones) until the rational brain is engaged.

of shame" down the echoing center aisle to the back of the church with a tantrumming toddler.

The amygdala is not a static structure of the brain. It functions more akin to a muscle. Just as lifting weights will increase the size of our muscles, being in a state of fight or flight actually causes the amygdala to grow.[52] When we experience threat mode (fight or flight) over an objectively nonthreatening situation—for example, if we see a small gray object in a dark corner of the pantry and immediately scream and slam the pantry door—our amygdala will take that as confirmation that the threat was *very real*. The next time we see what might be a mouse, we will have an even greater reaction. Each time we react like this, the amygdala is growing, being primed to act even more like that in the future. In this way, it hijacks the rational brain—which could have identified the small gray object as the harmless child's bath toy that it actually was.

As we've discussed, it's actually necessary for the amygdala to be able to hijack our rational brain; in the case of a true threat, it needs to have command of all the resources necessary to escape. But you can guess by now what happens if your perceived threat is not actually a threat and yet you respond as though it *is* a true threat: The amygdala grows larger, seeing the need for even more vigilance and hyper-responsivity. This can lead to that constant state of stress and 24-7 threat mode that Naomi was experiencing.

In most cases, after the threat is over or the prefrontal cortex has judged the situation to be nonthreatening after all

---

[52] Sara Gottfried, *Brain Body Diet: 40 Days to a Lean, Calm, Energized, and Happy Self* (New York: HarperOne, 2019), 235.

(for example, when we think we see that mouse in our pantry and scream, but then realize it was actually just a toy), our adrenaline and other stress-related hormones will dissipate. But for some people—like Naomi, or someone who has suffered trauma—the hormones do not return to baseline. Instead, they remain heightened, vigilant, and ready to respond at any moment.

At the same time that your amygdala sees the need to respond to your perceived (or imagined) threats growing larger, and so grows larger itself, the rational brain can actually *shrink* in size. Being in a constant state of stress causes a continual release into the brain and body of stress-related hormones, including cortisol. Cortisol releases glucose into the bloodstream—which is important, useful, and legitimately helpful when facing a true threat. But it also slows other functions, ones that are not essential to survival. And eventually, too much cortisol can prevent the stress response from turning off at all, like a strained and tired muscle that is continually engaged in a painful cramp: "The combination of heightened stress and high cortisol also shrinks your brain, damages your hippocampus, decreases brain activity, causes cognitive impairment, and increases your risk of other medical conditions, including anxiety disorders."[53]

Anxiety doesn't just grow in an individual; it's also contagious.[54] Here in the state of Virginia, for example, we often go into a collective panic when the weather forecast suggests snow. As the first fluffy white flakes begin to drift over the nation's capital, traffic immediately snarls and backs up,

---

[53]   Ibid., 237.
[54]   Brewer, *Unwinding Anxiety*, 22.

accidents happen … and soon there is no milk or toilet paper on the grocery store shelves. Yes, the otherwise highly intelligent, arguably politically astute, high-achieving inhabitants of this part of the country completely turn off their rational brains and go into survival mode.

TAKING CHARGE OF YOUR AMYGDALA

The first step in learning to deal with (and perhaps even eliminate) anxiety is simply becoming aware of what triggers our anxiety and how the brain functions on anxiety. Learning how uncertainty can trigger anxiety is an important part of learning how to deal with anxiety. When Naomi became aware of how ruminating over all the negative possibilities put her into threat mode, and how the surge of adrenaline in the middle of the night prevented her from being able to sleep—and when she realized that ruminating was not the same thing as effective and productive planning—she was able to begin developing strategies she could implement during the daytime as well as at night to stop the anxious thoughts. She began to train her mind to understand and acknowledge that not all uncertainty or ambiguity needs to be seen as threatening; but her rational brain needed to be engaged in order to dispel her impending and all-too-active anxiety and ruminating.

One of Lianna's clients, Susan, had previously struggled with episodic anxiety. Shortly after having her first baby, she reached out again to Lianna.

"My baby is one month old, and I'm feeling really, really overwhelmed! I don't know if this is just typical postpartum hormones and the transition from zero kids, but I'm just having a Really Hard Time!" she explained. "I keep having these terrible thoughts: What if I drop the baby? What if I roll over on him at night accidentally? (And I don't even co-sleep!) What if he stops breathing? I'm worried he's not getting enough milk. I google everything all the time.

"I'm probably being silly," she continued, "because doesn't every new mom stress about these things? Plus, my hormones are a mess and I'm not sleeping—for obvious reasons!"

"You did the right thing in reaching out," Lianna reassured her. "If the thoughts are bothering you, that's significant." It's important to remember that even if what you're experiencing is considered quite normal, if it's causing issues, then it *is* a problem worth addressing.

In responding to some follow-up questions, Susan shared that she was having significant difficulty sleeping—not just because she was up all night nursing but because, after she would put her baby down, she would stay awake watching the baby monitor, or checking and double-checking that the Owlet device—a "smart sock" that provides real-time monitoring on a baby's vitals and sleeping patterns—on her infant son was working. It seemed like every moment was consumed with worries for his safety: fear of sickness, fear of SIDS, even fear that she would cause harm to her baby on purpose. She didn't want to leave the house, but she was afraid to be left at home alone with him.

Sleeplessness and worry about every little thing related to the baby (is that a rash? did the baby sleep enough? did the baby sleep too much?) are normal, to a certain extent, but the frequency and intensity with which the worries come and the degree to which they impair normal functioning are what make them significant. Parents of newborns are notoriously sleep-deprived, but not being able to sleep even in the small windows available, because anxiety keeps you awake, is a sign of postpartum anxiety. It's not simply that you have many concerns about the new baby but rather that your worries become all-consuming, and the worry itself negatively impacts you. For Susan, it was affecting her sleep and her appetite, and was even causing heart palpitations.[55]

Though some anxiety with a new baby is normal, *this* degree of anxiety was not normal or to be expected. As with Naomi, it was clear that Susan needed to do something to take charge of her amygdala. So together with Lianna she made a plan[56] to resume individual therapy on a weekly basis. They reviewed the coping skills she had used in the past that she could try to implement again (e.g., keeping a gratitude journal, putting her phone away after a certain time at night to avoid doomscrolling during late-night feedings, and practicing mindfulness as a way of calming herself and peacefully becoming aware of the present moment).[57] Because she'd had positive experiences with medication in the past, she also made a plan to talk with her OB about going back on an

---

[55] Applying the DSM-5-TR criteria for an anxiety disorder would exclude those who experience excessive worries postpartum for less than six months; thus some researchers define perinatal generalized anxiety disorder if the illness meets other DSM criteria for a minimum duration of one month. Shaila Misri et al., "Perinatal Generalized Anxiety Disorder: Assessment and Treatment," *Journal of Women's Health* 24, no. 9 (2015): 762–770, https://doi.org/10.1089/jwh.2014.5150.

[56] Making a plan is different from ruminating and worrying; the latter can cause anxiety and discouragement, whereas a plan uses the prefrontal cortex and takes one out of threat mode.

[57] We discuss mindfulness in depth in chapter 9.

antidepressant medication that could be taken while breast-feeding. Though having a new baby is hard, it doesn't necessarily need to be as hard as Susan's mind and body were making it.

For some people, medication for anxiety can be lifesaving, and it can actually be vital to restoring proper function of the amygdala. The proper medication can bring their experience of anxiety or depression down to a manageable level so that they can utilize coping skills and practices such as those we will recommend in this book. Medication also benefits some problems more than others. For a number of disorders, it is a first-line intervention (e.g., any disorder where psychosis is present). At the same time, for many types of anxiety, such as general anxiety disorder, there is good evidence supporting the use of therapy along with pharmacological interventions. And then, of course, for specific phobias (the most common of all anxiety disorders), therapy alone is the recommendation. In some cases, such as obsessive-compulsive disorder (OCD) happening concurrently with depression, a combined treatment is an effective approach.[58] Whatever you do, make sure you have a real conversation with your care provider about the risks and benefits of any medication you might be considering.

As therapists, our default is to seek behavioral ways to help clients change and grow; however, we have witnessed the powerful and beneficial impact that medications can have. Psychopharmacological treatments generally do not work as

[58] Irismar Reis de Oliveira, Thomas Schwartz, and Stephen M. Stahl, eds., *Integrating Psychotherapy and Psychopharmacology: A Handbook for Clinicians* (New York: Routledge, 2014), 125ff.

simply and directly as antibiotics for an infection. Finding the correct type of medication and the correct dosage with the fewest side effects is much more complicated than that. And even if a medication does bring about symptom relief, that's only one aspect of healing. Making changes in our lives that result in the formation of new and more healthy habits is almost always a part of any anxiety cure.

One of Lianna's clients recently described the experience of taking prescribed medication as having blinders removed. Prior to taking medication, her vision had been focused only on everything bad in her life; ever since starting medication, she has felt as though her field of vision has widened. Now, in addition to seeing the bad, she can also feel and see what is good in her life. The good things in her life had all been there before, but she hadn't been able to focus on and feel them. Medication helped her find the freedom to not be trapped in the negative thoughts, to break out of dwelling in the pain, and to begin to do the hard work of therapy, changing the way she viewed and experienced the world.

Remember that there is no shame in turning to your medical doctor for advice on the appropriate medication for your situation. Perhaps you've heard that humorous story about the man who was clinging to the roof of his house after a massive flood, praying to God to save him from drowning. A man in a rowboat came by and offered to rescue him, but the man on the roof refused to go with him, saying, "No, thank you. God will save me!" Then a motorboat came by, and the captain called out to the man on the sinking house, offering to take him on his boat. But again, he responded, "No, thank you! I have faith in God!" Later, a helicopter sent down a rope ladder for him to climb to safety, but the man clung to the roof of his house, refusing the ladder, stubbornly insisting, "God will save me!" Eventually, the floodwaters rose over him, and the man drowned. Upon reaching the pearly gates, he asked God, "Why didn't You save me?" God replied, "I tried! I sent you a rowboat, a motorboat, and a helicopter." God often asks us to use the ordinary means available to us in order to heal us—and sometimes being saved from drowning in anxiety means taking a first simple step to finding the right medication.

In the Acts of the Apostles, we can read the beautiful and heartwarming story of the man who was lame from birth. He is hoping for alms, but he receives so much more—and from an ordinary man, one not yet a saint, the very man who had denied Jesus three times and yet became our first pope:

> And a man lame from birth was being carried, whom they laid daily at that gate of the temple which is called Beautiful to ask alms of those who entered the temple. Seeing Peter and John about to go into the temple, he asked for alms. And Peter directed his gaze at him, with John, and said, "Look at us." And he fixed his attention upon them, expecting to receive something from them. But Peter said, "I have no silver and gold, but I give you what I have; in the name of Jesus Christ of Nazareth, walk." And he took him by the right hand and raised him up; and immediately his feet and ankles were made

strong. And leaping up he stood and walked and entered the temple with them, walking and leaping and praising God. (3:2–8)

Not only does God work through ordinary, fallible humans, but He also gives us the great commission to "go into all the world and preach the gospel" (Mark 16:15), to encourage each other daily, to build one another up in charity, and to give all the honor and glory to Him. And, more than that, to do so joyfully, walking and leaping and praising God.

CHAPTER 3

Fear of the Podcaster

*Today, many people are plagued with diffuse
fears: fear of failure, fear of falling behind, fear
of making a mistake or a wrong decision, fear of
not meeting one's own standards. This anxiety is
reinforced by a constant comparison with others.*

—Byung-Chul Han[59]

*What is so frightening to so many people about
speaking to an audience?… Is it because you fear a
total failure of performance such as never happened
in the history of the world, so that not one word will
come to your mind and world chaos will follow?*

—Walker Percy[60]

*Heart pounding, palms sweating, mind racing.
As my breath becomes quick and shallow, I feel
as though I've been running miles. I ask myself,
why am I feeling this way? There's nothing to*

---

[59] Byung-Chul Han, *The Expulsion of the Other* (Cambridge: Polity
Press, 2018), 32.

[60] Walker Percy, *Lost in the Cosmos: The Last Self-Help Book* (New
York: Farrar, Straus & Giroux, 1983), 30.

be afraid of! I'm just sitting in my living room,
awaiting a phone interview for a podcast.
—Laraine Bennett

WHAT'S IN A PODCAST?

For Laraine, embarking on a several-months-long round of interviews to promote and discuss one of her books gave rise to an unusual (for her) experience of rather intense (though episodic) run-ins with anxiety. Sometimes she would wake in the middle of the night with recriminating thoughts about how she needed to do more research and better prepare for the upcoming interviews—thoughts that would eventually keep her awake for an hour or two. These first thoughts would soon be accompanied by further unhelpful thoughts: Surely by staying awake, she would be even less prepared for the upcoming interview, as sleep deprivation would make her less capable of answering questions on the fly. Then, on the day of each interview, her heart would race, her palms would begin sweating, and thoughts of panicking while live on the air, of being unable to speak, or of saying something stupid raced through her mind. Breathing techniques didn't seem to calm her down. At one point, Laraine asked Art to try to help her relax, but when he suggested in a soothing voice, "You're an expert on this; you've done so much research," all she could think was, "I'm not an expert; I know nothing! I shouldn't be talking about this at all!"

When Laraine told their daughter Lianna (yes, the third co-author of this book!) about this new anxiety, Lianna decided to avoid the strategy Art had taken of offering supportive words. She decided to sidestep, saying such things as, "Mom, you've got this! I've heard you in interviews—you're always so good!" Instead, Lianna asked Laraine if she could respond to her on a more professional level. For reviewing purposes, they recorded the following discussion:

> Laraine: "Every time I'm scheduled to go on a podcast or do a radio interview, I feel so stressed out and have so much anxiety!"

> Lianna: "What exactly do you mean by *anxiety*?"

> Laraine: "Well, I feel my heart racing, my palms are clammy, sometimes my chest tightens, my breathing changes. … I just feel anxious!"

> Lianna: "Well, these are all bodily sensations."

> Laraine: "Oh, that's true! But I also experience dread, a sense that something terrible will go wrong—and this is in my mind."

> Lianna: "What are you worried will happen?"

> Laraine: "I'm worried they'll ask a question and I won't know the answer, or I'll go completely blank, or—even worse—I'll say something stupid."

> Lianna: "So you're not so much worried about the interviewer asking a question; you're worried about your response."

> Laraine: "Yes, that's it. I'm worried I'll say something incorrect or, worse, something completely stupid."

Lianna: "And, this may sound a bit silly, but what would be so bad about that?"

Laraine: "Well, the publisher is depending on me to do a good job. Also, the listeners are counting on me to say something enlightening. But instead, they might be thinking, 'Who is that stupid woman, thinking she can talk about St. Thérèse?'!"

Lianna: "What's so bad about looking stupid?" [Note that what sounds like a silly question is a technique therapists will use to "peel back the layers" to understand what might be at the root of someone's anxiety. Being anxious about an interview is a pretty common experience, but in order to help Laraine move past the anxiety, Lianna wanted her to explore what might be causing the anxiety in her unique circumstances. What is the underlying fear beneath the fears in this case?]

Laraine: "Well, I don't want to sound stupid. Who wants to be stupid? And I'm going to do a podcast with a woman in Australia, and I might end up alienating the entire continent. That would be very bad!"

Lianna: "Well, nobody goes on a podcast saying, 'I couldn't care less!' A little bit of anticipation, a heightened sense of energy, a little extra adrenaline, the extra blood flow to the brain — it all helps us think a little quicker on our feet. So this is natural and good. But the question is, your level of the fear or anxiety, is it proportionate to the event? The fear that you're going to embarrass yourself, is that even a legitimate fear? Yes, you might stumble over your words, or you might not give the best answer. But is that going to be an embarrassment that matches the degree to which your body is responding?"

Laraine: "Probably not. I'm curious: Why is my anticipation so negative? Why am I not excited about the upcoming interview? Why can't I keep the good part of adrenaline to be alert and on my toes? Instead, I label it as bad, and I have anxiety."

Lianna: "If your thought, 'What I say today will ruin my career,' were true, then that degree of anxiety might be appropriate. The question is, is it likely that anything you say during this podcast could have the actual potential to ruin your career? And the answer to that is that it's highly unlikely. And that helps keep the level of anxiety proportionate to reality. Also, if we focus on the negative aspects of the physical symptoms of heart racing and not being able to catch our breath, then those negative thoughts will escalate our anxiety. While we may not be able to immediately regulate our breathing or heart rate, we can practice thinking the thoughts to de-escalate the anxiety: 'Yes, my heart is pounding, but that's just my sympathetic nervous system sending blood to my brain to help me think quickly on my feet.'"

UNDERSTANDING THE DISTINCTION BETWEEN FEAR AND ANXIETY

Fear is one of the most necessary emotions to our survival. Every animal experiences fear. Someone once said we're all alive today because our ancestors had post-traumatic stress disorder (PTSD). Meaning, their fear and survival instincts worked as they are supposed to. When the saber-toothed tiger ate their friend, they knew that they should *run*—and avoid saber-toothed tigers going forward. Those who didn't have that fear response didn't survive.

As previously mentioned, the *Catechism* says, "By his emotions man intuits the good and suspects evil" (*CCC*, 1771). It also tells us, "The apprehension of evil causes hatred, aversion, and fear of the impending evil" (*CCC*, 1765).

We have automatic responses, often fear induced, that are lifesaving. We have this system whereby we learn really well what can hurt us, and we learn to be afraid of that. The good news is that, for most of us in this present age, we're not encountering this mortal danger in our daily lives. In his study of anthropology, Lianna's husband read a theory that some people are night owls because, back in the day when we were living in caves, someone had to stay up all night to be the watchman for the safety of the group. Now, however, although we have socially evolved past needing someone in this role, we have not evolved on a biological level—and so the person who stays up all night is said to have insomnia. Is this a leftover watchful fear from a bygone era, or is it modern-day anxiety? Well, what's the difference between the two? Here we'll return to Laraine and Lianna's discussion:

> Lianna: "Fear is a physiological response to a threat. There are also emotional components to this: It's happening in the brain—and in the body that will help you get away from what will harm you. We do experience threats, but in our lives today we can end up reacting to modern-day stressors emotionally as if they were life-threatening situations. This fear response is triggered, but it's out of proportion to the situation. When this fear response is out of proportion to the situation, that's what we call anxiety. This nonclinical, low-grade anxiety [i.e., fear that is out of proportion to the situation], dread, and the like sometimes keeps you awake at night and permeates the days you have an interview. But when you peel back the layers and take a look at what you're actually afraid of, what do you find?"

> Laraine: "Well, I guess I fear utter and total embarrassment, letting my publisher down, hoards of people slamming me on the Internet."

> Lianna: "All of which is very unlikely to happen. When you experience this fear, it should have been at a level three rather than a ten. That

difference is what makes the anxiety. There is always a fear underlying anxiety. There are times when fear is appropriate. However, anxiety is never appropriate. It is by nature a disordered response. Anxiety is either out of proportion to the situation or it is completely unhelpful. Anxiety can paralyze us. Does this make sense?"

Laraine agreed that it makes sense.

Lianna: "In the case of the podcast, a certain physiological response is actually helpful: the increased blood flow, the adrenaline, the heightened senses … all these can actually help you to be more responsive and quick thinking while answering questions! Adrenaline is helpful and keeps you sharp. Anxiety, on the other hand (or the perception of anxiety), can actually paralyze you and prevent you from doing your best.[61] So, perhaps by reframing your feeling of nervousness, increased heart rate, and the like as simply the adrenaline you need to be fully alert and on your toes to answer all questions, you can dial down the level of 'anxiety' from an inappropriate ten to a more reasonable three. And, secondly, reminding yourself that the worst that can happen is not actually life-threatening, but perhaps only a mild blow to your ego, can also help turn down the dial."

[61] You will discover that anxiety itself can be positively reframed as adrenaline.

Did this discussion immediately reduce Laraine's anxiety when anticipating an upcoming podcast or radio interview? No. She still doesn't look forward with happy anticipation to podcast interviews. The effects of positive impacts are often more subtle than a complete about-face. But this discussion did, in fact, "turn down the dial" of her anxiety level.

REFRAMING THE THREAT LEVEL

Not only does reframing any anxiety-inducing situation help dial down the level of anxiety, but the brain itself is capable of learning and adapting to situations based on how we consciously react to them. Understanding how the amygdala works actually helps us respond to the perceived threatening situations differently, so that we can train our amygdala to decrease the level of anxiety.

As we mentioned in the preceding chapter, the amygdala (our smoke detector) responds to a possible threat by sounding the alarm: Get ready to fight, flee, or freeze! But the amygdala is also able to learn (for future reference) what are serious threats. Imagine if a caveman, like Bill Murray's character in *Groundhog Day*, had to relearn every day that a saber-toothed tiger was a dangerous threat to his survival! He would soon be a tiger meal. Instead, however, the amygdala learns what is a threat by "observing" your reaction to the sounding of the alarm. The more Laraine allowed herself to respond with heightened alarm at every podcast interview (for example, imagining the grumpy, nit-picking listener, or focusing only on ways she had previously messed up in an interview), the more the amygdala learned that this was, indeed, a serious threat.

When a toddler is just learning to walk, he falls seventeen times per hour for more than one hundred falls per day![62] If, when he first falls, everyone around him reacts with intense alarm, and proceeds to metaphorically or actually encase him in bubble wrap, his amygdala would immediately ramp up the threat level. "I guess it's really dangerous," his mind would tell him. "I need to increase my threat response." And the toddler, instead of just falling and getting up again, would cry and scream. As we grow up, so much critical learning requires ignoring the alarm sounding: the first day of preschool, the first time we have to present a project in front of our class, the first time we shyly ask someone to dance, and so on. These milestones are crucial, and each time we work through the fear, we grow stronger. Applying this by analogy to her own situation, Laraine can learn that by calmly engaging her rational brain, by calmly assessing the threat level, she can help to train her amygdala to understand that this situation (i.e., her podcast interview) is not threatening.

As part of the primitive brain, the amygdala has very few ways of learning about what constitutes a threat. Words and rational thoughts are not part of the primitive brain (hence the toddler having a meltdown that is a product of the amygdala hijacking the brain may not be comforted or instructed by words). The amygdala instead looks for signs of *approach* or *avoidance*. If you avoid the threat (fight, flight, or freeze

[62] Karen Adolph et al., "How Do You Learn to Walk? Thousands of Steps and Dozens of Falls per Day," *Psychological Science* 23, no. 11 (2012): 1387–1394, http://www.jstor.org/stable/23484542.

response), the amygdala learns that this situation is, indeed, a threat. And it will sound the alarm even more the next time it recognizes the same situation. This is called *threat learning* or *sensitization.* If, on the other hand, you allow yourself to calmly approach the possible threat while the alarm is sounding, the amygdala learns that it might not have been such a serious threat after all, and it will sound the alarm a bit less the next time. This is called *habituation* or *desensitization.*[63]

The key, then, to reducing anxiety stemming from a particular perceived threat is to approach that threat while the alarm is sounding. When Dusty Baker, a great baseball manager, managed the Washington Nationals and a relief pitcher had a bad game, or a utility fielder muffed a ground ball, he would put them into the very next game so they wouldn't perseverate over a mistake, but would instead focus on the business at hand: today's game. He didn't want his players to have any opportunity to incur a drop in confidence or to feed a negative internal processing bias. He knew that he could keep them positive by immediately getting them to go back out there and face the batters. When the amygdala saw the other players out on the field immediately after a bad game, it had a chance to realize that it didn't have to sound the alarm in that situation. In short, the players learned that they had opportunities to grow rather than experiencing the whole situation as a threat to be avoided.

This strategy of desensitization is actually used very successfully with cases of phobias—such as fear of heights, airplanes, or public speaking. Many people have been able to

---

[63] Kevin Majeres, "Master Class Lesson 20: Top Down Neuroscience," OptimalWork, https://optimalwork.com.

overcome their severe anxiety and panic attacks that accompany a particular situation (like flying) by gradually desensitizing themselves to it. You might not know that most phobias are actually about nonthreatening situations.[64] Most snakes or spiders, for example, are not life-threatening. Heights, public speaking, and small spaces are not life-threatening. Curiously, people rarely develop phobias over things that actually are dangerous, such as driving, drinking, and guns. The significance of this is that we rarely fear (in the sense of a dramatic phobia) those things we're familiar with and have dealt with: Our amygdala learned to accept these (sometimes actually dangerous things) because we lean into them rather than avoid them.

In Laraine's case, reframing her threat response (racing heart, sweating, anxious thoughts) as adrenaline that can help her be alert and on her toes to better answer the interview questions—and *facing* the anxiety-provoking situation (the interview) instead of fleeing (telling the publisher she couldn't do the interviews)—helped her become more comfortable with the interviews.

Dr. Kevin Majeres, psychiatrist at Harvard Medical School and co-founder of OptimalWork, tells us that if you can identify the exact point where the challenge is most negative, then you have identified the exact place where the most growth can occur.[65] In Laraine's case, that point was

---

[64] Jonathan Haidt, *The Anxious Generation: How the Great Rewiring of Childhood Is Causing an Epidemic of Mental Illness* (New York: Penguin Press, 2024), 74.

[65] Kevin Majeres and Sharif Younes, "How to Learn to Love Anxiety," *The OptimalWork Podcast*, episode 49, https://optimalwork.com/the-podcast.

immediately prior to the phone calls that started the interviews. Though she may have worried in the middle of each preceding night over whether she had prepared enough for the call, or whether she was even worthy of talking about St. Thérèse, her anxiety would reach its most acute point immediately before the phone calls. So she started taking several deep and calming breaths, reframing her nervous feelings as an energy that heightened her ability to answer questions. "Adrenaline," she would say to herself, "will bring blood to my brain and help me be more focused and intelligent during the interview." And she would try looking at it from a new perspective, asking herself, "What is the worst that can happen in this interview? Fumble the answer to a couple of questions?" She would even focus on thinking positive thoughts about the interviewer, such as, "She really is a sweet person who simply wants to share a message of universal sisterhood!" With each of these tactics, she would begin to lessen the level of the threat that her amygdala was experiencing. And of course this, in turn, had the overall effect of lessening her level of anxiety.

This may not work the very first time, or perhaps not even the first five times! Learning a new process and adapting ourselves to a new habit of thought does take time. And at first, our amygdala will cry foul because it has been assigned the task of alarming us. It will do what it has been trained to do! But eventually, as we continue to embrace the challenge with a positive attitude, our amygdala will decrease its alarm, and our anxiety will be dispelled.

PRACTICE THE PAUSE
(THIS REQUIRES VIRTUE!)

1. The next time you experience a surge of anxiety, fear, or panic, instead of running away, pause.

2. Take a deep, calming breath (inhale through the nose; exhale in a deep sigh).

3. Note the increase of adrenaline. Ask yourself: Can it be turned to something positive? Can I use it to be more sharp and attentive? What can I learn from this situation?

4. Ask yourself: Can I face the fear and anxiety with a calm, rational attitude?

Chapter 4

Wired to Worry?

We believe that the temperamental biases we call high- and low-reactive in infancy and inhibited and uninhibited in children are due, in part, to distinct neurochemical profiles in the amygdala.

—Jerome Kagan and Nancy Snidman[66]

Temperament or Environment?

As young moms, Lianna and her sister Lucy were both dealing with two-year-olds and nursing babies—toddlers and babies who needed naps (and, just as important, their moms needed them to nap!). The sisters noticed a marked difference between their approach to nap time. Lianna was hyper-focused on maintaining a nap schedule, making sure the firstborn went down for a nap at the proper time and observing carefully the "wake windows" because "sleep begets sleep." She used blackout curtains and had the crib set up in a dark and quiet room with a white noise machine. Lucy, however, let her babies fall asleep wherever and whenever, usually in her arms, for short power naps, never allowing nap schedules to dictate the day's activities.

---

[66] Jerome Kagan and Nancy Snidman, *The Long Shadow of Temperament* (Cambridge, MA: Belknap Press, 2004), 48.

How did these two diametrically opposed methods come about in sisters who had been raised by the same parents and who, growing up, were first homeschooled and then attended nearly identical schools? In other words, environment itself may not explain the difference here, but something else might.

In another example, Art and Laraine shared the case of "Nora" in their book *The Emotions God Gave You*.[67] Nora was a stay-at-home mother of three small children, and she was feeling consumed by anxious and sometimes self-recriminating thoughts. The dishes were piling up, the house was a mess, she couldn't make simple decisions such as what to cook for dinner, and the kids were constantly fighting. Nora felt overwhelmed by her chaotic life. What made matters worse, in her mind, was that her sister-in-law had five kids and a successful home-based business, and was still able to get in her weekly tennis games. When her sister-in-law would come over to visit, she would swoop through Nora's house, tidying and organizing everything she could, and she would even bring Nora's family a meal.

A crucial difference, though, between Nora and her sister-in-law was their temperaments. Where Nora was from childhood a sensitive, thoughtful, slightly anxious introvert, her sister-in-law was an energetic, optimistic extrovert who thrived on challenging situations. When Nora's sister-in-law was faced with chaos, she turned into General Patton and started rallying the troops. In the same situation, Nora wanted to surrender and cry.

---

[67] Art and Laraine Bennett, *The Emotions God Gave You: A Guide for Catholics to Healthy and Holy Living* (Frederick, MD: The Word Among Us Press, 2011), 29ff.

And Lianna and Lucy? They also are of very different temperaments.

Temperaments from Birth into Adulthood

Harvard psychologist Dr. Jerome Kagan (1929–2021), one of the pioneers in developmental psychology, extensively studied temperament and emotions. Kagan, once a strict behaviorist, was alerted by his own longitudinal studies to the existence of temperament. Early in his career, Kagan had been convinced that the environment—a child's parents, the quality of his education, his culture, and his access to resources—was all that mattered in terms of personality. Kagan absolutely did not believe in inborn traits or characteristics contributing to one's personality. A baby was essentially a blank slate on which the environment would write its future. However, he continued to notice, throughout several projects, that certain characteristics could be explained only by acknowledging certain biological, inborn—in other words, temperamental—characteristics. He was further intrigued by psychiatrists Alexander Thomas and Stella Chess, who studied temperamental characteristics such as mood, energy, distractibility, adaptability to new situations, sociability, and the like. Dr. Kagan decided he had to do his own longitudinal study on temperament.

Beginning with infants as young as four months old, he tracked temperament through adolescence. Could a baby's responses to novel stimuli predict their future personality? Would infants who were easily upset or more likely to cry in new situations grow up to become more anxious and shy? It was not hard to determine which infants were more upset, as these poor babies would thrash their arms and legs and would cry and arch their backs[68] if they were upset by unexpected images or heard unfamiliar sounds.

Approximately five hundred infants were fed and rested before being shown unfamiliar sights, sounds, and smells. They saw brightly colored Winnie the Pooh mobiles, heard voices coming from a speaker, and smelled diluted rubbing alcohol—none of these were intrinsically scary; rather, they were simply novel. Most of the babies just watched or babbled and remained relatively still in their infant seats. But one baby, Baby 19, was different. "She was distressed by novelty—new sounds, new voices, new toys, new smells—and showed it by flailing her legs, arching her back and crying. Here was what Kagan was looking for but was not sure he would find: a baby who essentially fell apart when exposed to anything new."[69] He dubbed these sensitive babies "high-reactives."

This baby was more easily upset, but would she continue to respond with such sensitivity as she grew older? Was Baby 19 "wired to worry"?

Kagan's hypothesis was that the differences among the responses to unexpected situations or sights were due to their

---

[68] Arching the back was an important clue for Kagan; this unique response is actually caused by the amygdala—indicating a more excitable amygdala. Only 20 percent of all infants tested showed this response. Jerome Kagan, *The Temperamental Thread: How Genes, Culture, Time and Luck Make Us Who We Are* (New York: Dana Press, 2010), 30.

[69] Robin Marantz Henig, "Understanding the Anxious Mind," *New York Times Magazine*, September 29, 2009, https://www.nytimes.com/2009/10/04/magazine/04anxiety-t.html, accessed October 2, 2023.

different biology, which affected their arousal threshold; he further speculated that these temperamental differences would continue as they grew older. In fact, this turned out to be the case. Baby 19 became timid and anxious, while the "low-reactive" babies were more easygoing, social, and spontaneous.

At fourteen months, and again at twenty-two months, Baby 19 became easily distressed when placed in a strange room, when introduced to new toys, or when an unfamiliar person entered the room. Like Baby 19, all of the children in the original study were interviewed throughout childhood and up to adolescence. By age seven, half of the highly reactive babies had fears of dogs, thunder, darkness, or social situations. And fifteen years later, in a follow-up interview, Dr. Kagan found Baby 19 to be shy, anxious, and worried about many things. An MRI at age eighteen showed that not only was her amygdala highly reactive, but her prefrontal cortex (which regulates emotion) was even notably thinner than that of other high-reactive children from the study, suggesting that Baby 19 would be even more prone to anxiety than other highly reactive children.[70] Most of the high-reactive children did well in school, despite the fact that they reported being very stressed out before exams, sometimes even vomiting from nervousness, and having trouble sleeping.

In short, what Dr. Kagan discovered was that the highly reactive, sensitive infants had a "biologically prepared tendency that [makes them] vulnerable to worry."[71]

It is important to underscore this point: We are not *determined* or *inescapably destined* by this biological *preparation*.

---

[70] Ibid.
[71] Kagan, *Temperamental Thread*, 12.

Rather, it simply makes us more or less vulnerable to worry and anxiety. By the same token, someone who tends to be flexible and easygoing is not immune from ever experiencing anxiety or worry.

NATURE VERSUS NURTURE

Psychologists have long debated the primacy of either nature or nurture—that is, the extent to which biology or experience shapes each person, and whether one factor outweighs the other—and, for many years, Harvard psychologist Jerome Kagan had come down firmly on the nurture side. He initially believed that education would solve all social ills, and that personality had nothing to do with inborn traits. He had even scoffed at his own mother, who always insisted that our personalities were the result of inborn traits. Babies, asserted Dr. Kagan, were essentially blank slates—tabula rasa—upon which life experiences were written, thus shaping their personalities.

Kagan first began questioning his firm belief in the exclusivity of experience (nurture) when he participated in studies that clearly implicated certain physiological features in differentiating timid children (who also became timid adults)—these timid children had highly reactive sympathetic nervous systems.[72]

He was also influenced by the child psychiatrist team of Drs. Alexander Thomas and Stella Chess, who challenged prevailing behaviorist theories with a seminal New York longitudinal study that spanned thirty years and studied nine temperament-related characteristics: activity, rhythmicity,

[72] Ibid., 3–7.

adaptability, approach or withdrawal in new situations, threshold of responsiveness, intensity, mood, distractibility, and persistence.[73]

And so he eventually began his own longitudinal research study, starting with those five hundred infants at four months of age, and continuing through adolescence, focusing on a single observable temperamental characteristic: each infant's reaction to unexpected or unfamiliar events.

Readers might be nonplussed by Kagan's original position as a staunch behaviorist—someone who believed that there was no such thing as an innate characteristic that could determine an infant's (and, later, an adult's) personality. Every parent, in opposition to Kagan's first stance, has the common-sense belief that babies are born into the world with their own little budding personalities. And then life's experiences are added to the mix. Nature + nurture = personality. Lianna herself has marveled that she and her husband, both cautious introverts, gave birth to an extrovert—a rambunctious, fun-loving baby who can't get enough of people and activities. Yet it took scientific studies—actual research—to convince Jerome Kagan of the truth about temperament.

What Is Temperament?

Temperament is that part of our inborn nature that, through biological tendencies to react in certain ways, serves as the *building blocks* of our future personality. Our total personalities and our characters are comprised of much more than

---

[73] Stella Chess and Alexander Thomas, *Temperament in Clinical Practice* (New York: Guilford Press, 1986), 288.

temperament—which is why we always have the possibility of growing in virtue and changing for the better. Temperament never *programs* us to respond in any particular way, nor does it confine us to a box. Rather, it gives us a tendency to lean in a particular direction. Some people tend to react more quickly and intensely, while others do not. Some people are more or less sociable in new situations. Some are easily aroused, while others are very laid-back. Some people are more wary of new situations, while others jump in feetfirst. Some people love to immediately take charge, while others just want to fit in and go with the flow. From birth onward, we might be sensitive, tranquil, or slow to warm up. These are all temperament differences that can have a profound impact on our emotional lives, on our relationships, and even on our spiritual lives (as Art and Laraine have discussed in their popular books on temperament from a Catholic perspective).[74] We are never determined to act according to our temperament, because, as unique individuals created in the image and likeness of God, we are always free to respond to God's grace and to grow in wisdom and virtue. But it is the challenge of a lifetime—as many saints have attested—to overcome certain temperamental tendencies and to grow in heroic virtue.

Differences in temperament can profoundly impact how each of us reacts to the individual circumstances of our lives. Depending on temperament, we might respond to a stressful

---

[74] See Art and Laraine Bennett, *The Temperament God Gave You* (Manchester, NH: Sophia Institute Press, 2005); *The Temperament God Gave Your Spouse* (Manchester, NH: Sophia Institute Press, 2008); *The Temperament God Gave Your Kids* (Huntington, IN: Our Sunday Visitor, 2012); and Know Thyself: The Game of Temperaments (Sophia Institute Press).

situation with anger or withdrawal. Depending on temperament, when confronted with an unexpected or new situation, we may be eager or fearful. And when thinking about a bad experience, one person might ruminate over it, replaying it over and over in their mind, while other temperaments brush it off and put it behind them.

With this in mind, it should come as no surprise that temperament can definitely impact our approach to anxiety.

Anxiety is a label that we place on a set of physiological reactions including increased heart rate and muscle tension. It is possible that one would experience these reactions and yet label them as something else: *excitement* (of the sort experienced while riding a roller coaster, for example) or *nervous energy* (in a positive sense, as before receiving a public award). Or perhaps even *energizing* if one uses the feeling of anxiety as a motivation to accomplish something.

A high-reactive amygdala is identified by increased heart rate and muscle tension *and* when these bodily experiences are *interpreted negatively as anxiety.*[75]

In chapter 6, we will discuss how life experiences can shape the way we interpret and respond to different situations (and, notably, how traumatic experiences have an outsize impact on our reactivity and future experience of anxiety). However, there is also our own unique biology—our temperament, if you will—that can make us more (or less) vulnerable to anxiety. Journalist and science writer Robin Marantz Henig discussed this in a 2009 *New York Times Magazine* article:

[75] Kagan, *Temperamental Thread*, 43.

Not every brain state sparks the same subjective experience; one person might describe a hyper-aroused brain in a negative way, as feeling anxious or tense, while another might enjoy the sensation and instead uses a positive word like "alert." Nor does every brain state spark the same behavior: some might repress the bad feelings and act normally; others might withdraw. But while the behavior and the subjective experience associated with an emotion like anxiety might be in a person's conscious control, physiology usually is not. This is what Kagan calls "the long shadow of temperament." The oldest high-reactive subjects in Kagan's and Fox's studies, like Baby 19, are in their 20s now, and for many of them, no matter how much they manage to avoid looking anxious to an outsider, fears still rattle in their skulls at 3 o'clock in the morning. They remain anxious just below the surface, their subconscious brains still twitchy, still hypervigilant, still unable to shift attention away from perceived threats that aren't really there.[76]

A hyperreactive amygdala, like a smoke detector whose batteries are malfunctioning, keeps sounding the alarm. For certain temperaments, that alarm means anxiety. Henig continues: "Maybe a high-reactive person with a jumpy amygdala can manage to avoid the behavioral and subjective experience of anxiety because of a strong cortex that can quiet the overactive brain. But in

---

[76] Henig, "Anxious Mind."

Baby 19's case, the jumpy amygdala might instead have been accompanied by a cortex less able to mount an inhibitory response. 'Maybe when those things occur together,' Schwartz said, 'your outcome is that you have a little bit more trouble.'"[77]

PUTTING IT ALL TOGETHER

Jerome Kagan discovered that the roots of anxiety can begin in infancy. He writes, "All the evidence supports the claim that unexpected events, especially if they are unfamiliar, activate an already excitable amygdala in children and adolescents who were high-reactive infants and renders them prone to anxiety in unfamiliar social situations."[78] However, with good parenting, social development, and education, children can learn to deal with their temperamental inclinations and manage their tendency to anxiety. Some of the highly reactive children discovered ways of managing their own anxiety as adolescents—for example, by following rules, exercising, or planning to dissipate anxiety. And Kagan himself said he always preferred high-reactive people as his research assistants: "They're compulsive, they don't make errors, they're careful when they're coding data."[79] By temperament, and reinforced by training, these research assistants are particularly conscientious and exacting—just what Dr. Kagan valued in research.

It's important to note that our Catholic Faith teaches us that, as we are all created in the image and likeness of God, we are always fundamentally free—free to choose to follow

---

[77] Ibid.
[78] Kagan, *Temperamental Thread*, 47.
[79] Henig, "Anxious Mind."

God's will (or not) and always free to respond to God's grace; we are never determined—whether by our own nature or by our environment. Thus, temperament will never force us to act in a certain way; it gives us a *tendency to react* in certain ways, but through our own growth in natural skills and in virtue, we can learn to respond in the most appropriate way, given the situation.

Art's client from chapter 2, Naomi, who was struggling with anxiety about the increased demands that her new job placed on her, was undoubtedly what Kagan would call a "high-reactive" and what Art and Laraine have described in their temperament books[80] as a sensitive melancholic. This means that she already had a predisposition or tendency to view life's circumstances through a slightly less optimistic lens. She approached new situations tentatively, and she had a little less natural self-confidence than a boisterous extrovert might. She was conscientious, perfectionistic, and careful with her work. She also knew that she was highly qualified for this position—and in fact she wanted to grow in her career and also personally through stretching herself.

As she began to understand how her own temperament combined with the more challenging circumstances of her life to create anxiety, she was able to more effectively channel the nervous energy, the anxious thoughts, and the tendency to ruminate in the middle of the night. Understanding her own temperament also allowed her to give herself more grace, if you

---

[80] See *The Temperament God Gave You* (Manchester, NH: Sophia Institute Press, 2005); *The Temperament God Gave Your Spouse* (Manchester, NH: Sophia Institute Press, 2008; and *The Temperament God Gave Your Kids* (Huntington, IN: Our Sunday Visitor, 2012).

will, to acknowledge that she was by nature more likely to slide into worry, and then to take steps to prevent the anxious thoughts from spiraling out of control into full-blown anxiety.

Art introduced one way to reduce anxiety (more on this in part III), suggesting that she consciously make a *plan*. Often when we're ruminating or worrying, we believe that we are, in a sense, planning. But we're not. Worrying and ruminating can put us in threat mode. When we develop a plan and a strategy, however, we're using our prefrontal cortex, which takes us out of fight or flight.

One of Lianna's clients, Audrey, faced a similar conundrum that had brought her into therapy. She was embarking on a major life change: She was engaged to be married. Significant life changes, such as getting engaged to be married, are a common reason to turn to therapy. In addition to being highly detail-oriented, organized, and conscientious by temperament, Audrey was also a successful wedding planner.

Audrey realized two things: First, she wanted to enjoy her engagement and wedding; and second, she also was the one and only person she trusted to manage the process. Given her tendency to "murder the details," she was facing a conundrum. Her mom and her maid of honor had eagerly offered assistance in planning and managing details, but Audrey didn't believe they would be able to accomplish these to her level of exactitude or stick to her timeline. Lianna was able to help Audrey devise a way of maintaining a sense of control while not negatively impacting her enjoyment of the process. Remember that devising a plan and developing a strategy are not the same as ruminating or worrying. Once a strategy has been devised, the brain can relax its need to "solve this problem *now!*"

Temperament also impacts whether we have a tendency to approach a strange or new situation (even as babies, as in Dr. Kagan's famous experiments), to withdraw from it, or to do neither. The same will be true in potentially threatening situations, where the individual by temperament will tend to approach (fight), withdraw (flight), or do neither (freeze). According to Dr. Judson Brewer, individuals who tend to be more motivated by the hope of good outcomes (for example, getting a raise) tend to approach (fight when the amygdala is activated); those who are more motivated by fear of negative outcomes (for example, fear of being reprimanded) tend to withdraw or avoid (flight when the amygdala is activated). Those who are very easygoing will tend to freeze.[81] For example, Naomi's habit of worrying about her work situation was actually her way of motivating herself—fear of making a mistake, missing a deadline, or being called out was motivating for her. Nonetheless, ruminating and worrying are not the same as developing a strategy for action. Once a plan or strategy has been set in motion, we can get off the hamster wheel of ruminating and take positive action.

[81] See Judson Brewer, *Unwinding Anxiety: New Science Shows How to Break the Cycles of Worry and Fear to Heal Your Mind* (New York: Avery, 2021), 95ff.

HOW TO STOP RUMINATING IN THE MIDDLE OF THE NIGHT

And which of you by being anxious can
add one cubit to his span of life?
—Matthew 6:27

Art, by temperament a worrier, was once told by his Carmelite spiritual director that if he wakes in the middle of the night and begins to ruminate and worry, he should pray the Rosary. Art, being a bit of a perfectionist, objected that it wouldn't be a "good" Rosary! Nonetheless, praying the Rosary can be a soothing way to take your mind off worrisome things, take you out of threat mode, and place you in a calm, meditative mindset that is more suitable to sleep. Some people find that simply holding a rosary helps them get back to sleep. Even Pope Benedict XVI struggled with severe insomnia; some believe this was one of the reasons he stepped away from the papacy. He revealed the depth of the struggle: "These are the cares and duties to which we are exposed every day from dawn to dusk and which so fill our mind and heart that they pursue us into our sleep."[82]

---

[82] Pope Benedict XVI, *The Yes of Jesus Christ: Exercises in Faith, Hope, and Love*, trans. Robert Nowell (New York: Crossroad, 2005), 120.

If, like Naomi and Art and even Pope Benedict, you struggle with ruminating in the middle of the night, you might also try the following:

1. Take a deep breath through your nose. Breathe in yet again. Hold for a few seconds. Slowly exhale. Repeat as necessary. It may take a few minutes to achieve a sense of calm.

2. If the intrusive thoughts still bother you, you can write them down to worry about the next day. Another suggestion is to refrain from focusing on them; instead, unfocus your eyes (even with your eyes closed) as though viewing these thoughts from a fuzzy distance. Practice distancing your mind from your thoughts during the day so you can do it more easily at night.

3. Let the thoughts float away like a cloud or a balloon. Do not engage the thoughts by responding with another thought, arguing with a thought, or entertaining a thought in any way. Simply let the thought drift away.

CHAPTER 5

Isn't Some Anxiety Good for You?

*"A little anxiety helped me get started on writing the
book that I've been procrastinating on. Having a
deadline makes me anxious, and I think that helps!"*

*"A little anxiety before giving a
talk means I'm on my toes."*

*"Worrying about being late means I plan
ahead and am always on time!"*

STRESS: A NECESSARY PART OF LIFE?

Paul briskly entered Lianna's office wearing a stylish Italian suit and checking his expensive watch. "I'm sure we can sort this out quickly, because I really don't have much time," he began.

After inviting her new client to sit down, Lianna said, "You mentioned when we spoke on the phone that your doctor recommended talking to someone about your anxiety. Can you tell me a little bit more about that?"

"First off, I don't have 'anxiety.' I just have a stressful job. I've been to the ER three times now for chest pains. I assumed it was a heart attack; my dad died of a heart attack at fifty, so it was a possibility. But they checked me out and there was nothing. Then it happened again, a week after that. This clenching in my chest, racing heart, trouble breathing. I thought they missed something the week prior. But same thing: no problem with the heart. The doc says it was a panic attack. I've literally never been in a 'panic' in my life! It's the most absurd thing. I have stress, but it's a part of the job.

"What I don't have time for," he went on, "are these 'panic attacks.' I can't be rushing to the ER every week, wasting my time just for the doc to tell me I have anxiety. I need this to stop."

"It sounds like you're used to managing high-stress situations, but something is going on where suddenly your body isn't handling the stress like it used to be able to. Has anything changed for you recently?" Lianna asked.

Paul insisted that he never felt any anxiety and had no idea what might have triggered the so-called panic attack. Stress just came with the job, and he loved his job. He wasn't trying to reduce his level of involvement at work or decrease stress, but his doctor had told him that he had to do something, or he'd continue to experience what the doctor was calling these panic attacks. He initially saw no particular trigger for the attacks; they just came out of nowhere.

Paul viewed himself as a man who shouldered all of his own responsibilities and then some, a man who was calm in the face of the ongoing demands of a high-powered position. And he knew that stress was simply a part of that job, so how was he supposed to "reduce stress"?

Until the alarming experiences that mimicked heart attacks, Paul would actually have said that he "thrived on stress," that it motivated him to work harder and better — perhaps even that he couldn't do his job well without it.

His story, then, presents us with two questions: Do some of us thrive on stress? And isn't stress a necessary part of life?

A World without Stress: Is It Possible?

In the dystopian society imagined in 1931 by Aldous Huxley when he wrote *Brave New World*, the populace was subdued by behavioral conditioning and through a drug: Soma. Strong emotions were seen as a threat to the World State's dominance and mission of Community, Identity, Stability. Everyone needed to be in a state of "happiness" — it was not true happiness, however, but rather simple pleasure. Mustapha Mond, the leader of the State, said, "People are happy; they get what they want, and they never want what they can't get.... They're blissfully ignorant of passion and old age." This was a dystopian world — a world with no anxiety.

A 2005 science fiction movie, *Serenity*, directed by Joss Whedon, adds a twist to the dystopian theme. The intrepid crew of *Serenity*, a spaceship, lands on a mysterious planet, Miranda, which is supposedly a new utopian earth. Instead, they find dead bodies everywhere. A hologram from a long-dead doctor on that planet reveals her discovery: The governing body on the planet had infused its entire atmosphere with a drug, "Pax," which was supposed to create a peaceful, anxiety-free world, with no anger or aggression. But it had instead lulled the entire planet to death.

Jerome Kagan, the Harvard psychiatrist we quoted previously, speculates that, without the anxiety T. S. Eliot suffered from, he may not have been able to write his great works of poetry, most notably the melancholic epic *The Waste Land.*

On the other hand, Sylvia Plath, also a renowned poet and author, committed suicide at the young age of thirty. Author Joyce Carol Oates said about Plath's poems that they "read as if they've been chiseled, with a fine surgical instrument, out of arctic ice."[83]

Thinking of all these examples from art and literature, of what was produced from various states of mental unrest—and what might happen when we try to eliminate that disquietude entirely—we might start to wonder: Is a little anxiety good? How much is too much?

In Paul's case, even though he felt he "thrived on stress," and that stress was an integral part of his work, he began to realize, with the help of therapy, that in fact it was beginning to take a toll on him and on his relationships. His initial refusal to even consider the potential impact of stress actually served to paradoxically increase its effect.

Art had a client who voiced a similar attitude, someone used to working long hours in a very high-stress job but whose spouse finally said, "Enough. I think you need to see someone about your workaholism."

"*Workaholism?* It's called 'supporting the family'!" retorted Art's client.

Nonetheless, he did eventually come in for therapy, even if somewhat ambivalently, because, in addition to his wife's insistence that he was "overdoing it" at work, he was beginning to

---

[83] Joyce Carol Oates, "Raising Lady Lazarus," *New York Times,* November 5, 2000, https://archive.nytimes.com/www.nytimes .com/books/00/11/05/reviews/001105.05oatest.html.

experience symptoms such as difficulty sleeping. At first he made the case that these symptoms were probably just due to his growing older, but he allowed for the slight possibility that they might be connected to his work schedule. Nonetheless, he insisted that stress and overwork were the way it had to be. This was his mindset because, though he knew himself to be intelligent and well educated, he was working in a city and in a career where everyone else in his peer group was better educated and even more brilliant than he was, so he had to try harder than all the rest of them. This meant, or so he thought, that he needed to work longer and harder than all those around him.

Art shared with his client that he, too, used to view things this way—until he began to get high blood pressure and some autoimmune symptoms. He suspected these were signs of overwork and stress, and that he needed to find a way to deal with the stress rather than deny it.

Both for Art and his client, as well as for Paul, rather than accepting "stress" as a necessary fact of life or even viewing it benevolently as an impetus to productivity and success, it would be better to understand in each situation that being busy and productive is a good thing, but being *stressed, burned out*, and *overwhelmed* can land you in the hospital.

Art described for his client the situation where the saber-toothed tiger is about to pounce, and the amygdala comes online to flood the body with stress hormones, increasing blood flow to the extremities, preparing the body to take action, getting the heart racing, the breath shortening, and overall readying to fight or flee. The entire body (and the brain) is in threat mode in this type of situation: tense, adrenaline pumping, on high alert.

Art asked him, "Does this experience sound familiar to you?"

His client nodded. "That's me, 24-7."

In Paul's case, Lianna carefully walked him through the details of his life, asking him to take note of the elements of any situation that occurred immediately prior to any panic attack. Specifically, she asked him to take note of when (and where) in his body he experienced the impending panic.

Art, too, asked his client where *he* felt the anxiety in *his* body. At first, neither Paul nor Art's client could pinpoint a place. But then they both said, "I think it's in the chest."

EXISTENTIAL ANXIETY

In his difficult (and perhaps controversial) book, *The Christian and Anxiety*, Catholic theologian Hans Urs von Balthasar elucidates a theological interpretation of anxiety, something he says is necessary because modern man experiences existential anxiety to an unprecedented degree. In previous centuries, the culture supported and reinforced belief in the existence of God. But now modern man is surrounded by a culture in the throes of an existential crisis of faith, and therefore, unsupported by a believing community, each one of us faces a personal experience of mystery and the elusiveness of God. Furthermore, although Christ has overcome anxiety, individual man still struggles with sin and neurotic anxiety. Balthasar describes the very real tension between being a baptized Christian in the state of grace and yet being capable at any moment of falling into sin, as long as we are still pilgrims on our journey to Heaven. He gives this tension a name: anxiety. Are we not all conscious of our weakness, perversity, constant backsliding, and lukewarm attitude?[84] We might also speak of this tension as the state of fallen humanity living in a sinful, broken world.

And yet Christ has come to conquer all evil. In Christ's Passion and death on the Cross, He experiences the "absolute anxiety" — the source of all other forms of anxiety — in order to redeem it and transform it: "Anxiety is one of the authorities, powers, and dominions over which the Lord triumphed on the Cross and which he carried off captive and placed in chains."[85]

Commenting on this passage from Balthasar, scholar Anthony Cirelli notes: "What one learns from this is that God does not come to abolish anxiety, for it is a given of human existence as such, but rather comes to enter into it himself and therefore to be in solidarity with suffering humanity; and in this solidarity God transforms anxiety by giving humanity a perspective and orientation for overcoming it. The Incarnation of God, which signifies the promise of the mediator, alone gives meaning to anxiety, especially in the abandonment undergone on the Cross. Christ teaches that fear and anxiety are quite real when understood as separation from God."[86]

Balthasar continues, "The absolute anxiety, which undergirds and surpasses every other anxiety [presumably the anxiety

---

[84] Hans Urs von Balthasar, *The Christian and Anxiety* (San Francisco: Ignatius Press, 2000), 99–100.

[85] Ibid., 81. The fact that Christ conquers all evil, including the evil of anxiety, is not what is controversial about Balthasar. The controversial aspect is the extent to which the theologian claims Christ must enter into our human suffering and anxiety. Does Christ (who is God) experience the total absence of God?

[86] Anthony Cirelli, "Facing the Abyss: Hans Urs von Balthasar's Reading of Anxiety," *New Blackfriars* 92, no. 1042 (November 2011): 705–723.

of the Old Testament and of the New Testament, sin anxiety and neurotic anxiety], thus becomes the standard and tribunal for all. This anxiety is drained to the dregs upon the Cross."[87]

Nonetheless, the sickness that Balthasar calls "secular anxiety" does grip modern man. But *this* kind of anxiety—being afraid of death, withdrawing into the isolated self, feeling despair—is "forbidden" by Christ. Such anxiety is forbidden by Christ because the Christian needs only to *turn to God*, to make an "act of faith, in which he dares to place himself and the whole world in the hand of the One who can dispose of him for death and for life."[88] This, of course, is precisely what those of us dealing with anxiety are trying to do: to turn over this anxiety to the Lord, and to trust that He can help us do so.

"Christianity offers man, not a bottomless pit, but solid ground—grounding in God of course, and not in self. To place oneself on this solid ground involves relinquishing one's own ground."[89] And the more one turns from God, the greater the anxiety. In fact, as we shall discover from Bishop Conley's account of his anxiety and depression in chapter 9, it is not overtly "turning away" (because we may not have consciously done so) but rather being overly *self*-reliant that increases our anxiety. This existential anxiety can happen when we fail to fully face the fact that, as finite beings, we are radically dependent upon the infinite God.

And anxiety in the modern age is increasing especially as we rely less and less upon God; in fact, the more we place our

---

[87] Balthasar, *The Christian and Anxiety*, 75.
[88] Ibid., 90.
[89] Ibid., 99–100.

trust in ourselves, the greater the anxiety. Between ourselves and our Creator is a bottomless chasm, and sin (or being overly dependent on the self) refuses to walk in the pathway of God: "The uneasy conscience that many Christians have, and the anxiety based on it, do not come about because they are sinners and backsliders but because they have stopped believing in the truth and efficacy of their beliefs."[90]

Anthony Cirelli comments on this: "One can only say with Balthasar that the origin of anxiety is, and can only be, explained theologically as sin, that is, sin understood as the falling away from intimacy with, and trust in, the infinite God."[91] This "sin anxiety" (which can be the source of psychological anxiety) is the hell of God's absence.

Nonetheless, Balthasar asserts, "Any place from which the smoke of the abyss can rise up through the cloven earth is a place to which the light of salvation ... is able to penetrate."[92]

Perhaps the only truly proper or legitimate "anxiety" is "fear of the Lord": not "fear" in the usual sense of the word, but rather that reverence, awe, and honor in the face of the mystery, grandeur, and ultimate otherness of God. It is a holy trepidation, because we love Him, and so we do not want to sin. And if we do sin, our remorse is because we offend the One who deserves all our love.

In Balthasar's theological interpretation of existential anxiety, as with our garden-variety psychological anxiety, anxiety is experienced because there is no possibility of fully understanding the void between the infinite God and our

---

[90] Ibid., 100.
[91] Cirelli, "Facing the Abyss," 705–723.
[92] Balthasar, *The Christian and Anxiety*, 77.

finite selves. The only true "solution" is to turn toward God with confidence and love, as St. Thérèse would say, relying on Him alone. In this turning toward the mysterious infinitude that is God, we do face the dizzying abyss that is between us—an abyss that we cannot even cross by our own power. But it is only in turning toward the awesome (in the true sense of that word) mystery of the infinite God that anxiety will be dispelled; in this *turning toward*, Balthasar is not unlike contemporary neuroscientists who say that anxiety can only be overcome by leaning into it.

LEANING INTO ANXIETY

Harvard Medical School psychiatrist Dr. Kevin Majeres says, "I love anxiety."[93]

This may sound like an unusual statement coming from a psychiatrist who specializes in helping anxious patients.

Dr. Majeres shares the story of one of his clients, a pilot, who had been grounded by the Federal Aviation Administration.[94] He had been flying when his co-pilot began telling him, in gory detail, of a dental procedure that went wrong—and he passed out. It turns out—unbeknownst to the pilot himself!—that he had a needle phobia. More specifically, he had a

[93] Kevin Majeres and Sharif Younes, "How to Learn to Love Anxiety," *The OptimalWork Podcast*, episodes 49 and 126, https://optimalwork.com/the-podcast. Art took the OptimalWork Master Class and highly recommends it, as well as *The OptimalWork Podcast*, which can be found at https://optimalwork.com/.

[94] Kevin Majeres and Sharif Younes, "Overcoming Anxiety: Feel the Fear," *The OptimalWork Podcast*, episode 181, https://optimalwork.com/the-podcast.

blood-injection-injury phobia. He hadn't even been aware that he had this condition! But hearing those gory details triggered his quiet phobia, and that's when he passed out mid-flight.

Dr. Majeres said he was able to cure him of this phobia within just two or three sessions because phobias—which are really an intense experience of anxiety around a specific thing or situation (such as snakes or needles) are very treatable using exposure therapy. Specific phobias—an irrational fear of an object or situation—are, in fact, the most common of all anxiety disorders.[95]

Exposure therapy works by training the amygdala that the perceived threat (needles, in this case) is not actually a threat, thereby decreasing the threat response. The amygdala is trained through exposure to the threat itself. Exposure therapy (whether in vivo or virtual reality) is almost universally recommended due to its high success rate and widely positive effect.[96]

Where does the amygdala get the idea that something is a threat? It's difficult to pinpoint, and often it doesn't really matter. The pertinent information is that the amygdala got the message that something was a threat, and that thing was then avoided. But avoidance just heightens the sense that it's a threat. And each time you avoid it, you increase the anxiety, and the amygdala's alarm increases. The amygdala is identifying it *right now* as a threat. But as long as you welcome and approach it, you train the amygdala that it is not a threat.

[95] Irismar Reis de Oliveira, Thomas Schwartz, and Stephen M. Stahl, eds., *Integrating Psychotherapy and Psychopharmacology: A Handbook for Clinicians* (New York: Routledge, 2014), 127.
[96] Ibid., 128.

That's how you retrain your amygdala. "The more you try to bring anxiety on, the more it goes away," says Dr. Majeres.

The amygdala is always alert for avoidance behavior. It concludes that anything you avoid "must be a threat" and it begins to heighten the threat response. When the amygdala perceives avoidance, it sees the threat as even *more* of a threat. And when the amygdala senses the threat (needles, in this case), it begins to activate all the classic fear responses, such as increased (and then decreased) blood pressure, quick shallow breathing, and so on. As it happens, these two responses in particular can cause people to faint.

Dr. Majeres needed his patient's amygdala to learn that needles are not threatening. And here's the good news: The amygdala can be taught! When the phobic person encounters the threat—whether needles, snakes, airplanes, or something else—the amygdala is at its peak of anxiety. At that very moment, if you lean into the anxiety, you teach your amygdala that it's not a threat after all. As Dr. Majeres puts it, "You can only train your amygdala when it is firing!"[97]

The key is to *approach* the threat, rather than to withdraw from it, at the height of anxiety. With each successive attempt to approach the threat, the anxiety decreases more and more until it is at an "appropriate" level for the situation. An "appropriate" level of anxiety for public speaking, for example, might be to have just enough adrenaline to keep the speaker alert, eloquent, and quick thinking.

And this is why Dr. Majeres says he "loves" anxiety. It is not anxiety itself, per se, but the reframing of it as a helpful burst of

[97]   Majeres and Younes, "Overcoming Anxiety: Feel the Fear."

adrenaline that can be used as an opportunity to learn to train one's own amygdala to respond in more appropriate ways.

Dr. Judson Brewer, on the other hand, unequivocally states that there is no such thing as "good anxiety"—not even a little bit of it. To those who claim that a little anxiety helps their performance, Brewer questions whether they are committing the fallacious argument post hoc, ergo propter hoc: You may have performed well on a particular occasion before in which you had anxiety, but the correlation doesn't equal causation. In fact, research studies have shown that stress actually inhibits performance.[98]

Nonetheless, and most surprisingly given this stance, Dr. Brewer also encourages us to "lean in." He does frame it, however, in slightly different terms.

Curiosity,[99] he says, is a way to lean into a potentially threatening situation, rather than avoiding it. You can simply turn toward a thing that is unsettling, with a questioning and open attitude: "I'm curious; I wonder how I'm feeling right now. Oh, interestingly, it's more of a sense of alertness, and not actually anxiety or fear." Curiosity—or wonder—also takes us out of threat mode and sends us into the prefrontal cortex and growth mode.

With this lens in mind, we return to an earlier question: Is anxiety part of the human condition? If so, how much is

---

[98] Judson Brewer, *Unwinding Anxiety: New Science Shows How to Break the Cycles of Worry and Fear to Heal Your Mind* (New York: Avery, 2021), 82.

[99] Many spiritual writers caution us against curiosity because it can at best be a source of distraction and at worst lead us into sin. Here we are using curiosity as a detached desire to know or understand something, more akin to wonder.

"healthy," or at least permissible, and how much is destructive? Most psychologists will say that when a behavior begins interfering with your daily functioning, it has become problematic. That is, if I have the occasional burst of anxiety (say, before giving a talk in front of a large crowd), this is "normal" and to be expected. In fact, as Dr. Majeres would say, I can reframe that anxiety as adrenaline that's helping me perform at a peak level, with heightened senses and additional blood flow to the brain: "Anxiety is a high level of performance waiting to happen."[100]

But what if I have so much anxiety that I can't do the occasional talk that I've been invited to do? Or I wake up every morning with a black cloud of dread hanging over my head, with a sense of doom and destruction, or the feeling of brain fog and an inability to perform simple daily tasks? Or I'm avoiding flying to weddings because of a phobia of planes, or I'm landing in the ER due to heart palpitations? In these cases, I am in the land of anxiety that is neither normal, manageable, or within reason. Nor is it possible to reframe it as something productive. This is when I should take steps to alleviate it. The point of leaning into anxiety is not to go white-knuckle or encourage torturous angst. It is, rather, to reframe the obstacle of dread as an opportunity to grow and overcome challenges.

Once Lianna's and Art's clients learned to practice a calm awareness of the present moment, they discovered where in their bodies their anxiety was held, and they could begin to release that feeling by taking several long, deep breaths. The very act of breathing and being mindful can diminish the fear response, as we will discover in later chapters.

[100] Majeres and Younes, "How to Learn to Love Anxiety."

Even Hans Urs von Balthasar, focusing on the existential experience of anxiety, gazing dizzily into the abyss between the sinful, finite self and the eternal God, views the "solution" as leaning in — toward God. He presents a solution in taking the lead to walk with God and choosing to rely totally on Him, rather than in turning away and trusting only the self. Writing in his 2024 pastoral letter about his struggle with deep depression, a struggle that caused him to take a leave of absence from his diocese, Bishop James Conley shared some personal and very relevant insights: "It was during this period of darkness that Jesus' words, 'Apart from me, you can do nothing,' began to take on deeper meaning. As I more fully embraced the Lord as healer and teacher, I learned more about my radical dependence on Him. I started to experience the freedom of surrender as I gradually allowed Jesus to shoulder burdens I had been carrying on my own."[101]

---

[101] Bishop James Conley, "A Future with Hope," Diocese of Lincoln, May 2024, https://www.lincolndiocese.org/afuturewithhope.

CHAPTER 6

Trauma and Anxiety

My heart is in anguish within me,
the terrors of death have fallen upon me.
Fear and trembling come upon me,
and horror overwhelms me.
—Psalm 55:4–5

For the reasoning of mortals is worthless,
and our designs are likely to fail,
for a perishable body weighs down the soul,
and this earthy tent burdens the
thoughtful [anxious] mind.
—Wisdom 9:14–15

The anxiety becomes so acute that the brain can't
… well, in the absence of any better words, I'd say
that the brain doesn't have sufficient bandwidth to
process all the information. The firewall collapses,
so to speak. And anxiety overwhelms us.
—Fredrik Backman[102]

---

[102] Fredrik Backman, *Anxious People* (New York: Simon and Schuster, 2019), 79.

JANICE: FROM CHILDHOOD TRAUMA TO ADULT ANXIETY

"I can count on one hand the number of times my parents were nice to me."

Janice, one of Lianna's clients, was talking about her childhood. She was one of the younger children in a large, chaotic family, and she had suffered neglect and physical abuse from her parents.

"Once, I was so sick I couldn't go to school, and my mom bought me a McDonald's kids' meal. It was the nicest thing she had ever done for me. Most times when I was sick, they just told me to shut up and stop whining. Once, when I broke my arm at the playground, it was three days before they took me to the doctor. When the X-ray showed it was broken, my dad told me I 'had it coming' because I was 'so stupid.'"

And then, sure enough, he switched back to the familiar refrain and told her to shut up and stop whining.

Arguments about finances, living paycheck to paycheck, Dad's tendency to drink heavily and then become physically and verbally abusive, and Mom's helplessness and constant yelling all combined to create a home atmosphere that was chaotic and neglectful. One of Janice's siblings avoided their turbulent home life by staying out late with friends, drinking, and eventually getting into trouble with drugs. Janice attempted to avert Dad's wrath and Mom's constant criticism by performing well in school. Nonetheless, despite her efforts as a child to "make her parents happy" (or at least to avoid being a constant target), her parents remained indifferent to her at best and abusive at worst. She heard, "Don't cry, or I'll give you something to cry about," a lot more often than, "I love you." She learned that nothing she could do — even getting the best grades — would earn her parents' esteem and love. In her heart, she began to believe that it was indeed all her fault, that she was just a worthless human being.

As an adult, Janice struggled with very low self-esteem, a tendency to make poor choices in relationships, and troubles at work. She internalized parental messages that she was stupid and worthless, which resulted in her frequently undermining her own efforts to perform well. It didn't help that one of her bosses reminded her of her dad: angry and punitive. The only home she knew growing up was radically unsafe; consequently, she sought out adult relationships that were equally unsafe. Nor did she ask for help, because in her experience, showing weakness only invited further abuse.

She showed poor judgment when dating, and she chose men she would later discover were alcoholics, or drug users, or verbally or physically abusive. In other words, she had one long string of losers. She would stay in each of these relationships far longer than any healthy person, because there was a large part of her that believed she was mistreated because she didn't deserve anything better — she was so stupid, she thought, and nothing but a problem. She *wanted* better from her relationships but never believed she *deserved* better.

*When I was a child, I spoke like a child, I
thought like a child, I reasoned like a child.*
—1 Corinthians 13:11

The way that children (especially under the age of seven) cope with the unfortunate, painful, or traumatic circumstances of their lives is to blame themselves.[103] And there is a protective factor in this mindset: "If it is my fault that bad things happen to me, then maybe I can do something to prevent this in the future." That thought gets encoded. We rational adults reading this book know that a five- or six-year-old is never responsible for the parents' divorce or the death of a loved one. But a child does not know this. "If Mom doesn't appear to love me," a young child thinks, "it must be because I am *unlovable.*" But the truth may be that perhaps Mom had a mental illness and was struggling with depression, and that's why she hid in her bedroom instead of caring for her daughter.

Trauma is a very sticky thing. An experience happens to a person, but rather than containing that experience and moving on from it, a part of us, either mentally, physically, or emotionally, gets stuck living in that past event. To a part of our body and brain, it's as if the traumatic event is still happening. Maybe it's an image we can't get out of our head, maybe it's a sound, or a physical sensation, or a smell, or maybe it's what the trauma "taught" us about ourselves and the world. Trauma differs from a bad experience because the beliefs about ourselves that come through this experience are

---

[103] Francine Shapiro, *Eye Movement Desensitization and Reprocessing: Basic Principles, Protocols, and Procedures*, 2nd ed. (New York: Guilford Press, 2001), 44.

carried throughout our lives—even into adulthood if, like Janice, we experienced that trauma as children.

A Constant State of Alarm

Russell Kennedy, a doctor who specializes in anxiety, writes, "When we are separated from our attachment figures [parents], either physically or emotionally, our bodies go into a state of alarm.… This state of alarm, which started as a reaction to a real or perceived separation, becomes intensified and prolonged by the anxious thoughts of the mind. Over time, if we are subject to an alarming state of affairs (e.g., abuse, loss, abandonment, or rejection) we are unable to resolve, or if we don't have access to a caregiver that can love and calm us, that alarm state becomes stored in our body."[104]

The Unsolvable Problem

Not everyone internalizes a bad or negative event, or even a serious incident, as a trauma. Not all veterans experience wartime trauma. Many Vietnam veterans, for example, do have PTSD, but not solely because of what they experienced in Vietnam. For many of them, the traumatic impact was intensified by the environment on the home front at the time; when they returned home, they encountered anti-war protests and were greeted with the opposite of the wartime hero welcome that veterans of World War II received. How a person's family and community respond to an event can influence whether or not that individual processes

[104] Russell Kennedy, *Anxiety Rx* (Sioux Falls: Awaken Village Press, 2020), 4.

it as a trauma—even more than temperament, though that certainly has a role. It would be natural to think, "The worse the event, the more traumatic," but that's not actually the case. This is, perhaps, counterintuitive. We tend to think the component that makes an event traumatic is its violence or egregious nature; however, an incident in which, for example, a child is groped by an uncle can in fact be more traumatic, and can cause more lasting negative impact and harm, than a violent rape, depending on how it was handled by significant family members or the community. If the family doesn't believe the child who reported the assault and instead supports the abuser, or acknowledges that it happened but blames the child for the incident, it is almost guaranteed that the child will experience it in a traumatic way. Ultimately, how families and communities respond can impact how the person will or will not process the event as a trauma.[105]

The goal of trauma-processing therapy is not to erase what happened, but rather to reprocess it as a "bad event" as opposed to a "traumatic memory." A bad event can be filed away and stored in the long-term memory. A traumatic memory, on the other hand, does not get filed away. For the person who experienced it, and is still experiencing it, the memory is stuck in the present moment—some people experience this as flashbacks—because there is something about it that "doesn't make sense." When the brain has a problem to solve, it creates anxiety in the present. The brain is constantly

---

[105] Ibid., 111. Also see Casey Calhoun et al., "The Role of Social Support in Coping with Psychological Trauma: An Integrated Biopsychosocial Model for Posttraumatic Stress Recovery," *Psychiatric Quarterly* 93, no. 4 (2022): 949–970, https://doi.org/10.1007/s11126-022-10003-w.

trying to solve the questions "Why did this happen? Why did it happen to me?" Because we don't have answers, because it is an insolvable problem, we're constantly on the alert, being hypervigilant to potential threats. The traumatic event can't be filed away in long-term memory as a "bad event." Instead of "getting over it," we replay that traumatic event over and over, disrupting our present lives.

We have all had the experience of trying to recall *the name of that guy in that movie*. We rack our brains and finally give up in frustration. Hours later, just as we lay our head on the pillow, the name erupts from our subconscious: *Dennis Quaid!* Although our conscious brain had set the problem aside, all day long our unconscious mind was working on it. How much more conscious and unconscious brain activity is spent on "solving" the unsolvable problem of the traumatic memory!

When our son (Lianna's brother) Ray was ten or eleven years old, he tried to do a backyard stunt, hoping to send his bike soaring over a ramp; unfortunately, his "ramp" was a giant pile of mulch. Instead of soaring into the air, the front wheel of his bike got stuck in the mulch, and Ray flew over the handlebars, broke his arm, and had to be rushed to the emergency room. Ray didn't experience this mishap as a traumatic event, because it makes sense: If you fly over your handlebars, you will likely break a limb. It *could have become* a traumatic memory, depending on important people's responses. If we, like Janice's parents, had blamed him for doing such a stupid stunt, ignored his pain, or shamed him for it, then he could have taken on core beliefs that he was a bad or stupid person. But our parental response was appropriate: We calmly took him to the ER, expressed concern over his pain, chastised him a little for not wearing a helmet—and years later, we can all laugh about it.

When a potentially traumatic event occurs, very common initial reactions might include exhaustion, confusion, sadness, anxiety, and so on—all quite normal. "This is because most trauma survivors are highly resilient and develop appropriate coping strategies, including the use of social supports, to deal with the aftermath and effects of trauma. Most recover with time."[106] However, there are some individuals who experience long-term effects that would warrant professional therapy—these effects might include experiencing excessive or inappropriate guilt over the traumatic event, justifications for the perpetrator's behavior (especially in a situation where the abuser was a close relative or caregiver), experiencing triggers and flashbacks, developing self-destructive behaviors, having intrusive thoughts and memories, and reexperiencing the trauma.[107]

When Ray looks back on the bicycle incident, his arm doesn't still hurt today. When Janice recalls breaking her arm in PE class, she hears the voice of her dad saying, "That's what happens when you're stupid and clumsy. Quit whining." Janice actually *feels the pain* in her arm, the anxiety in her chest, and the shame before her dad.

For many people who have suffered abuse, one of the pieces that contribute to being "stuck" in the trauma is the question "What did I do to deserve it?" But there will never be

---

[106] Center for Substance Abuse Treatment, "Understanding the Impact of Trauma," in *Trauma-Informed Care in Behavioral Health Services* (Rockville, MD: Substance Abuse and Mental Health Services Administration, 2014), https://www.ncbi.nlm.nih.gov/books/NBK207191/.

[107] Ibid.

an answer to this. This keeps the person stuck because they're asking a question that is unanswerable. There is nothing they did to cause it! So, in their adult life, they are always afraid of doing the wrong thing and saying the wrong thing, which would incur further abuse. Even though they might not be cognitively aware of the memory underlying all their adult fears, it is driving these thoughts. If someone was abused as a child and experiences a situation that sets off the alarm (as in Janice's case, it might be her particularly authoritarian—even though not physically abusive—boss who sets off the alarm), he or she will react as though back in that original situation. The brain may attempt to explain the unexplainable situation by saying, "You deserve this treatment because you're stupid," or "I'm sure I'm about to be fired because I always screw up."

This is what was happening with Janice: the unsolvable problem, the lack of a loving caregiver to whom she could turn to help her child self understand or with whom she felt safe—all this contributed to a near-constant internal monologue telling her, "I am in danger. I can't protect myself. I am a stupid, worthless person. I am always overwhelmed." These thoughts can become part of the core beliefs of the individual who has experienced childhood trauma, or even life-altering trauma as an adult.

Such words may have been the way Janice understood things as a child, perhaps the only way she could make sense of her situation as a young person. Now that she's an adult, her erroneous core beliefs and the accompanying anxiety hijack her ability to navigate life in a healthy way. Feeling like a failure, anxious, and overwhelmingly lonely, Janice reached out for therapy.

Lianna began helping Janice by exploring her childhood in detail, and in discovering and helping Janice identify and vocalize the messages that she had internalized as a child. Lianna asked her to think about her child self in a particular situation: Janice had been about the age of five and was crying during Mass. Her dad had angrily yanked her out of church and said, "If you don't stop crying, I'll give you something to cry about!" and then he smacked her across the face. Of course, five-year-old Janice cried all the more, and this just seemed to her to be proof of what her father had said: She was indeed stupid.

But a turning point in Janice's therapy occurred in the process of eye movement desensitization and reprocessing (EMDR), a type of trauma therapy we'll discuss in more detail in chapter 10, when Lianna asked Janice, "What do you think—as an adult—about that little girl? Was she a 'bad' kid who needed to be punished? What would you—as an adult—do with a child in this situation?"

"No," said Janice, slowly. "I think the child was just having a hard time at Mass. I would give her a hug and tell her it will be okay, and when she stops crying, we can go back to Mass."

As she was saying this, Janice started crying. It was the first time she had shown herself some compassion. It was the first time she had seen herself as *worthy* of compassion and love, as someone who had dignity as a human person.

ANXIETY ROOTED IN TRAUMA

Dr. Russell Kennedy suffered from decades of anxiety so intense that at one point he even contemplated suicide. Nothing seemed to work for him—whether cognitive behavioral therapy (CBT), prescription antianxiety medications, or anything else. He hoped that going to medical school and becoming an M.D. would solve his anxiety, but instead it intensified. It wasn't until he realized that his anxiety was his mind's response to the alarm stored in his body that he began to realize how he might cure it. His previous solutions were, as he described it, like bailing water from a sinking boat. You can do it that way, but you never get to the source of the problem, which is the hole in the bottom of the boat.[108]

"Anxiety," he writes, "is an adaptation to a stress (usually chronic) that was too much for your mind and body to bear."[109] Kennedy's anxiety was driven by his being unable to connect as a child to his bipolar/schizophrenic dad, who later committed suicide. He describes how the anxiety came to be stored in his body. As a young boy, whenever he turned to his dad for comfort or security (when, for example, he had been scared as a child or suffered some minor traumatic experience that children do), he found his father, who was severely impaired by his mental illness, unresponsive. And understandably, Kennedy was unable to calm himself as a child. As Kennedy explains, with his dad's mind

> too fractured for him to connect with me, my alarm level increased. This alarm energy became a chronic state in my body, where it would energize more false, worrisome thoughts in my mind. At the same time, the alarm energy would create a sense of my survival being threatened,

[108] Kennedy, *Anxiety Rx*, 98.
[109] Ibid., 8.

which would impair my brain's ability to recognize those thoughts as false. As a result, I would believe, or give power to, the false worries I had created, thus increasing the sense of alarm, which then created more worrisome thoughts. I was trapped in a feedback loop I call the alarm-anxiety cycle, where the alarm in my body generated anxious thoughts in my mind and those thoughts generated more alarm.[110]

TRAUMA CAUSES DISCONNECTION

One of the crucial aspects of trauma is that it robs you of the present moment. You're not only constantly brought back to the past traumatic event, but you're also hypervigilant for potential threats in the future.

Kennedy explains that when a child cannot connect in a healthy way to a parent—which can happen for any number of reasons, including because the parent is volatile, abusive, distant, cold, or mentally ill—the child feels the need to constantly assess the parent's emotional state to determine whether it is safe. Instead of developing a healthy sense of self-awareness and self-knowledge, the child must focus exclusively on assessing the *parent's* mood or situation. Lianna's client Janice had to continually be on the alert to assess whether Dad was going to fly off the handle and start hitting the kids, or whether Mom was going to shut down and retreat for days. Her entire focus was to be constantly on the alert, assessing the safety of the situation. She had no time to spare

[110] Ibid., 5.

to determine her *own feelings* in the present moment. As a result, she had never even considered the possibility (until encouraged to do so in therapy) that the way her parents treated her was not the way a small child—or any human person—ought to be treated.

The unpredictable, randomly violent dad and depressed mom who never intervened left Janice in a constant state of alarm as an adult—fearing that physical and emotional abuse could happen at any moment (because, as it happened without rhyme or reason in her childhood, so, too, could it happen randomly today). Whenever something began to go wrong, she would immediately revert to the blaming, shaming, and judging of herself. Because she was in a constant state of alarm, constantly in threat mode, she was also unable to critically analyze these thoughts as false. Furthermore, because Janice and others like her never developed a feeling of "safety" with their primary caregivers as children, they find in adulthood that they also do not have the ability to find a safe haven, emotionally speaking. And so that alarm is constantly sounding; they are ever on the alert. As one of Art's clients put it, "I don't know what it's like not to be anxious and not to feel threatened. Is there another way to be?"

No Words

Bessel van der Kolk, M.D., using emerging findings from neuroscience and attachment research to develop and study a range of treatments for traumatic stress, has spent his career researching how children and adults adapt to traumatic experiences. In 1984, he set up one of the first clinical and research centers in the United States dedicated to the study and treatment of traumatic stress in civilian populations. He is also the founder of the Trauma Center (now the Trauma Research Foundation) in Brookline, Massachusetts, and a professor of psychiatry at Boston University School of Medicine. Dr. van der Kolk used brain imaging to research exactly what was happening in the brains of people who were experiencing flashbacks to earlier traumatic experiences. As he expected, the amygdala would light up as the individual experienced the typical fight-or-flight responses. But van der Kolk also discovered that there was a significant decrease in a key speech center in the left hemisphere of the brain, a region called Broca's area. When a victim of trauma says they simply can't explain what is happening when they experience a flashback, or they have "no words," this literally may be the case. In one of his books, van der Kolk explains:

> Patients suffering from trauma often feel they are "hijacked by images, feeling, and sounds" from the past.... All trauma is preverbal.... Victims of assaults and accidents sit mute and frozen in emergency rooms; traumatized children "lose their tongues" and refuse to speak. Photographs of combat soldiers show hollow-eyed men staring mutely into a void. Even years later traumatized people often have enormous difficulty telling other people what has happened to them. Their bodies reexperience terror, rage, and helplessness, as well as the impulse to fight or flee, but these feelings are

almost impossible to articulate. Trauma by nature drives us to the edge of comprehension, cutting us off from language.[111]

In brain imaging, van der Kolk discovered that during flashbacks, only the right side of the brain would light up. The organizing left side of the brain, which "remembers facts, statistics, and the vocabulary of events," is impacted by trauma and has trouble sequencing and identifying cause and effect and often experiences the loss of executive functioning.[112] When something reminds a traumatized person of the past, it can seem to him or her that the event is actually happening *now*, in the *present moment*. A helicopter flying overhead can suddenly immerse the war veteran in the experience of war.

According to van der Kolk, the individual "may not be aware that they are reexperiencing and reenacting the past—they are just furious, terrified, enraged, ashamed, or frozen."[113] They feel as though they are in imminent danger, a state of paralyzing fear or even blind rage, sometimes resulting in dissociating one's mind from one's own body. This is a form of self-protection. The more traumatic the experience, the more likely there will be dissociation.[114] The person dissociates from his own body, retreating into his own mind. In some instances, a trauma victim may seem to

---

[111] Bessel van der Kolk, *The Body Keeps the Score: Brain, Mind, and Body in the Healing of Trauma* (New York: Penguin Books, 2014), 40, 43.
[112] Ibid., 45.
[113] Ibid.
[114] Kennedy, *Anxiety Rx*, 95.

have no recollection at all of the trauma, though his body still experiences the effects of it.

Ideally, we will calmly, prudently, and rationally assess danger and threats. But when the system breaks down, as it can with trauma, we over-detect danger and automatically go into fight-or-flight mode.[115] And with our speech centers malfunctioning in these scenarios, it can be extremely difficult to communicate our need for help, or even to let the people around us know what's going on.

*T*RAUMA VERSUS *TRAUMA*

Lianna likes to explain to her clients that there is *Trauma*, and then there is *trauma*. "Big T" Trauma is experiencing physical or sexual abuse, being the victim of a violent crime, living through combat situations, and the like. Those who suffered these sorts of trauma often experience nightmares, flashbacks, rage, and intrusive thoughts such as, "I'm powerless," or "I'm not in control," or "I'm worthless." But many people who have not suffered such traumatic incidents can nevertheless still suffer from similarly negative and intrusive thoughts, and may experience overwhelming anxiety.

Have you ever returned to a childhood home or a place you visited when you were young? You remember the place as huge, but in reality, it was quite small. That's because you perceived it through a child's eyes. Similarly, many of us have early childhood experiences that impact our present lives. This is what is called "little t" trauma, and it relates to our early childhood experiences that have not been sufficiently resolved

---

[115] Ibid., 63.

to become simply "bad memories" but instead still recur as anxiety in our daily lives. These experiences might include being bullied, having an incessantly hypercritical parent, having a parent who abuses substances, being forced to mature too quickly (for example, having to become a parent to younger siblings because your parents got divorced), or losing a loved one—or even losing a beloved pet. Though some of these "little t" traumas may seem minor to our adult minds (for example, a schoolmate's comment about one's weight), these events are experienced by the child as far more significant. Even a disparaging comment can result in a dysmorphic body image.[116]

This "little t" trauma, something that was too much for the small child to handle and for whatever reason the child was left to handle on their own—whether because the parents were neglectful or simply because they were unaware—becomes stored as an alarm in our bodies and resurfaces in the form of anxiety when we are adults. An analogy proposed by Dr. Kennedy that helps us understand this is to imagine that each child has a cupful-size capacity to handle these small emotional traumas that can and often do occur in childhood. But then something else happens, such as the death of a grandparent, and the cup runneth over.[117] The "little t" trauma that overflowed is stored in the body, later to be resurrected as anxiety. Because the trauma (whether big T or little t) was too much for a child to comprehend with his child's mind, the body tucks the alarm away, but only for a time. Over time, if there is no safe attachment figure to help diffuse the alarm—just as Janice had

---

[116] Shapiro, *Eye Movement*, 43.
[117] Kennedy, *Anxiety Rx*, 8.

no one to help her—this alarm remains stored in the body, continually surfacing in ways that are unhealthy.

At the core of all trauma is the fact that (1) there was an overwhelming emotional experience that was too much for the individual to handle or to understand *at the time*, and (2) there was (for whatever reason, intentional or unintentional) no loving caregiver who helped the individual make sense of it (or simply accompany them lovingly through it) at the time. The unresolved trauma is then stored in the body as an overly sensitive alarm affecting that person in one way or another for the rest of their life, until they are able to process and integrate it.

PART TWO

Unhelpful Strategies

Chapter 7

When "Solutions" Make the Problem Worse

*Highly reactive families are a
panic in search of a trigger.*
—Edwin H. Friedman[118]

*I'm not worrying—I'm warding off tragedies
by constantly anticipating them.*
—*New Yorker* cartoon[119]

*Why is it possible to learn more in ten minutes
about the Crab Nebula in Taurus, which is
6,000 light years away, than you presently
know about yourself, even though you've
been stuck with yourself all your life?*
—Walker Percy[120]

---

[118] Edwin H. Friedman, *A Failure of Nerve: Leadership in the Age of the Quick Fix* (New York: Church Publishing, 2017), 99.

[119] Paul Noth, "Warding Off Tragedies," cartoon, *New Yorker*, February 12, 2024, https://www.newyorker.com/cartoon/a26580.

[120] Walker Percy, *Lost in the Cosmos: The Last Self-Help Book* (New York: Farrar, Straus & Giroux, 1983), 1.

COPING—OR NOT?

We all have strategies for coping that we have developed throughout our lives—whether consciously or unconsciously—some big, some small, that we engage when we're faced with stress, loneliness, fear, anxiety, worries, past memories, or even just a bad day. It may be a relatively harmless coping mechanism when used occasionally (for example, watching a TV show to relax after a big day, going shopping to distract from work pressures, having a glass of wine to unwind, or scrolling through Instagram), but when these coping mechanisms are inappropriate to the situation, or when they get out of our control and begin to take over our lives, that's when we might have a problem. And sometimes our go-to solutions can actually make the original problem worse.

Both Dr. Kennedy from the previous chapter and Art's client from chapter 2, Naomi, who was facing stress after her promotion, had developed a habit of *worrying* as a coping mechanism for anxiety. Naomi's attempted solution—worrying—not only made the original problem worse; it actually became the bigger problem! Now she was lying awake every night, anxiously ruminating.

This was an ineffective coping strategy. In fact, it made things worse. The more she worried, the more severe her anxiety became.

Many of us find reading a great way to wind down and relax before bed, but even this can lead to negative results. Anna Lembke, for example, the author of *Dopamine Nation*, is a psychiatrist and the chief of the Stanford Addiction Medicine Dual Diagnosis Clinic at Stanford University. She had always loved reading. But in her forties, she discovered that she herself had developed an unhealthy addiction. She had, along with her women friends, been reading what seemed to be a harmless, if trite, book of fiction that many women in her circles were reading: a vampire romance. However, Lembke slipped quickly from reading to relax and unwind, to reading increasingly graphic romances, to reading what was essentially pornography. She became, as she put it, a "chain reader of formulaic erotic genre novels."[121] She began to stay up later and later at night, wasting more and more time reading books like *Fifty Shades of Grey* about sadomasochism and more. Instead of spending time with her family, or cooking, or even sleeping, she read more and more of this genre of terrible fiction. Finally, she realized she was addicted, and she knew she had to break the habit.

Many of us initially find scrolling through Instagram to be a soothing break from the demands of work or a way to combat the boredom of changing diapers and doing the laundry. Yet we all know by now, both through common-sense observations and perhaps even more clearly through various studies, that too much social media has profoundly negative effects.[122]

Comfort food, sugar, smoking, shopping, a glass of wine, television, working out at the gym, scrolling through the news feed—whether to de-stress, self-soothe, combat boredom, or forestall anxiety, these sometimes innocuous and sometimes not-so-innocuous habits can wind up having

---

[121] Anna Lembke, *Dopamine Nation: Finding Balance in the Age of Indulgence* (New York: Dutton, 2021), 14.

[122] University of Pennsylvania, "Social Media Use Increases Depression and Loneliness, Study Finds," ScienceDaily, November 8, 2018, www.sciencedaily.com/releases/2018/11/181108164316.htm.

the opposite effect we hope for. They don't solve the original problem we were facing, and they can become new and even bigger problems.

In fact, almost anything can become a bad coping mechanism; anything can be misused. Isn't this in part why the Desert Fathers, the first Christian hermits, left their families and towns to live in the deserts of the Middle East in simplicity and solitude? Known for their wisdom, humility, self-denial, and contemplative spirit, they sought to attach themselves to God alone—and, to do so, they tried to detach themselves completely from the world and all its distractions. St. Anthony of the Desert was in his thirties and had just received a large inheritance from his parents upon their deaths when he heard the gospel proclaimed: "If you would be perfect, go, sell what you possess and give to the poor, and you will have treasure in heaven" (Matt. 19:21). Anthony immediately took this to heart, sold everything, and left for the desert. He and the other men like him left everything to be alone in the desert because they understood how *easily* we human beings can become attached to any created thing—even a good created thing. And so they undertook this radical way of life in order to pursue holiness. And, in seeking God's will, they found His peace.

Of course, the vast majority of us faithful Catholics are not called to be hermits in the desert. Surely we can find virtuous ways to enjoy the fruits of God's creation without succumbing to the evils of addiction! What could possibly be wrong with having a relatively harmless (so long as we don't abuse it) coping mechanism for those really tough days?

WHEN HAS YOUR COPING MECHANISM GONE TOO FAR?

What is the difference between having a glass of wine and using wine to escape? Or watching a Netflix show to relax for an hour versus binge-watching because you just can't stop? Are you listening to an educational podcast, or are you addicted to constant input and noise? Are you constantly listening to something or entertaining yourself because you're afraid of being alone with yourself? Do you worry and complain because that's how you avoid facing your own shortcomings? Are you overcontrolling because you're afraid that everything will go to hell in a handbasket if you trust someone else to handle the situation?

As therapy progressed, Naomi (Art's sleep-deprived, anxious client) revealed that throughout her childhood she often felt abandoned, let down, and misunderstood. As a result, she formed a deep conviction that she couldn't count on anyone other than herself. As an adult, to manage this anxiety, she attempted to take complete control of every situation. To the dismay of her co-workers, especially those who reported to her, she would micromanage and be constantly critical. Even at home, she would be overcontrolling and fearful of what might happen if she ever relinquished that control. She was a helicopter mom who made her husband feel like he was the inept Homer Simpson in the family. Because of her constant criticism, everyone felt as though it were pointless to even try to please her, so they would all give up helplessly while she fretted and tantrummed about all the details.

Art asked her, "What's the fear underlying your need to take charge and be in control?"

Puzzled by the question, Naomi answered, "Well, that everything will be done wrong! I just can't count on other people to do things properly. On top of all my work stress, I feel like I'm the only one who can manage the house and kids."

"I see," said Art. "But what would happen if everything was done wrong? What is your fear about that?"

"Everything would fall apart! I would be blamed. It would be my fault."

"And—bear with me—is there a fear under that?" Art pressed the point.

"That's who I am!" Naomi exclaimed. "I'm the one who does everything and keeps it all running. If I fail at that, then what purpose do I serve? If no one needs me, no one will love me.... Then I'll be alone," she whispered.

ABANDONMENT AS THE ULTIMATE CORE FEAR

The core fear that Naomi expressed was developed over years of feeling let down, misunderstood, and loved only for her achievements. This led to her core defense that kept her from having to face the fear: She must outperform everyone and constantly be in charge in order to defend against the possibility of being let down or abandoned. The fear that she would be abandoned and alone was so horrifying to her that she avoided trusting people. By controlling everything, she wound up with disgruntled co-workers, an unhappy spouse, and helpless kids.

What is alarming about this scenario is that the core fear causing such behavior (the fear that she would be abandoned) was actually being fed by her core defense! Driven by her fear of abandonment, Naomi *pushed people away*! In doing so, her core fear was actually strengthened. The sad irony is that a maladaptive core defense only makes things worse.

Prior to becoming Pope Benedict XVI, Joseph Ratzinger wrote in his *Introduction to Christianity* that abandonment is ultimately at the root of all our fears. "The fear peculiar to man cannot be overcome by reason but only by the presence of someone who loves him.... One thing is certain: there exists a night into whose solitude no voice reaches; there is a door through which we can only walk alone — the door of death. In the last analysis all the fear in the world is fear of this loneliness."[123]

Our Lord Jesus Himself takes on the burden of this, our deepest fear; He goes down into "the abyss of our abandonment," as Ratzinger expressed it so poignantly. After His Passion and death on the Cross, "He descended into Hell," as we state in the Apostles Creed. Christ goes first into Sheol (in Greek, Hades), where all righteous men and women had dwelt after death since the fall of humanity and prior to Our Lord's opening the gates of Heaven and bestowing upon fallen humanity His life-giving grace. He personally goes into the pit of darkness, into our greatest fear — into death itself — and conquers it.

"Death is no longer the path into icy solitude; the gates of *sheol* have been opened," writes Ratzinger. Now there is "life in the midst of death, because love dwells in it."[124]

As we look more carefully at our own coping strategies, we may find that we, too, are avoiding facing a deep fear. It

---

[123] Cardinal Joseph Ratzinger, *Introduction to Christianity,* trans. J. R. Foster (San Francisco: Ignatius Press, 2004), 300–301.

[124] Ibid., 301.

may be like the fear of abandonment that Naomi struggled with. It may be the fear of being unlovable. These fears walk hand in hand. For if we are unlovable, then we will be abandoned and alone.

Control — or Catastrophe?

Remember Lianna's client Audrey, the wedding planner from chapter 4, who managed her anxiety by "murdering every detail"? Her coping strategy was to control; she was so excellent that she was a successful and sought-after wedding planner. It is said that Shakespeare penned the famous saying "Your greatest strength begets your greatest weakness." In Shakespearean fashion, Audrey learned this when she became engaged to be married and decided to be her own wedding planner. She realized that her potential enjoyment of her wedding might be at risk if she continued functioning at the high level of control she was accustomed to for other people's weddings. The myriad of tasks that faced her as she planned the wedding were overwhelming, and she didn't feel like she could accept help, precisely because this was her actual job. If anything was not up to her standards, it would reflect badly on her, as a professional.

But she also wanted to be sane and happy. And so it was at this point, feeling overwhelmed by the conundrum, that she turned to therapy.

"It's not that I don't have people offering to help, or that I don't want others to help. It's just that no one else seems to take things as seriously as I do. I'm worried they won't get things done on time or as thoroughly as I would want them done," Audrey explained to Lianna.

"So you want the help, but then you find yourself micromanaging the helpers, which creates more work for you. It would actually be less stressful if you could just do it all yourself," said Lianna.

"Yes, and I could do it, too, but I just know that if I actually want to enjoy my wedding day, I need to figure out how to let go of the control."

"So, what's the goal? To be married to your amazing fiancé, right?"

Audrey laughed. "Yeah."

"But instead of focusing on this, you're getting all stressed out about the song list, the canapés, and the guests' gift bags—nothing that would prevent you two from actually getting married. This might sound like a silly question for a wedding planner, but what would be so bad about all those things either being messed up or not happening at all?" Lianna asked.

"It feels like my reputation is on the line," Audrey explained. "Everyone expects this to be the biggest and best event ever, for every detail to be perfect."

"And why would it be so terrible if it weren't?"

"I feel like I would be letting everyone down, that I would be a disappointment," Audrey said, sighing.

What happened was that everyone else's *perceived* expectations—note that these perceived expectations existed in Audrey's mind, and were not necessarily what everyone was actually thinking or expecting—overshadowed what was actually most important, what was actually going on. The flawed strategy for managing anxiety threatened to usurp the most important thing—the wedding and their marriage.

There are as many ways we humans manage our anxiety as there are unique humans. And anxiety itself, as we discussed in chapter 5, is a part of the human condition. It makes sense that we'll have a natural tendency to find a creative solution (or just a solution) to alleviate the feelings of anxiety that are, at best, uncomfortable and, at worst, incapacitating. Having a reasonable (and not dangerous or problematically addictive) solution, such as relaxing with a good book or having a stress-reducing exercise routine, is welcome and recommended.

But hopefully you can see by now that when the solution becomes its own problem — or creates an even worse problem than the anxiety or fear we're managing — then we need to rethink our strategy.

OFFENSE AND AVOIDANCE: PAST, PRESENT, AND FUTURE

Another coping strategy is to go on the offensive. When your spouse accidentally pushes your buttons and asks, "What's for dinner?" a switch flips and you yell at him, "Why do you always assume I'm the one who has to make dinner? I have a job too! And on top of that job, I also have *another* job — I'm the only one keeping track of the kids' activities and homework, doing all the laundry, and managing the home. You never lift a finger!" And he replies, "Are you kidding me? Just yesterday, I took the boys to soccer and baseball practice! I work fifty-hour weeks! You act like you do everything! You just can't let go of control!"

Before you know it, you've launched into a "demon dialogue" — a fight you've had many times before, one you fall into like the dreadful habit it is, and that never ends well.[125] But you can't seem to stop it.

This is yet another instance of falling back into a radically unproductive, even destructive methodology. In this case, we're ignoring the present moment by offensively yelling about things that haunt us from the past and induce anxiety about the future, focusing on anything except what's right in front of us.

Lianna discovered how anxiety could hijack the present moment when she was preparing for the Baptism of her second child. In typical melancholic fashion, she had carefully thought out and prepared for every detail: The clothes for all family members had been laid out the night before, the diaper bag was fully stocked, everyone had been fed breakfast, she changed the baby for the fourth time, and her husband and mother-in-law were instructed on the event schedule in five-minute intervals. She had planned the food, arranged for a photographer, and checked the weather. Not two hours before the Baptism, the priest who was supposed to administer the sacrament suddenly became seriously ill and had to call the church to find an available priest. This massive change of plans didn't throw Lianna off her stride, not even a little bit. But when the family finally arrived at the church, Lianna discovered she had left behind a miraculous medal she wanted to have blessed. In the middle of the crisis and all the commotion, somehow this one tiny (and not very significant!) detail threatened to steal her joy and distract her from the momentous occasion of her baby's Baptism.

---

[125] Susan Johnson, *Hold Me Tight: Seven Conversations for a Lifetime of Love* (New York: Little, Brown, 2008).

Our avoidance of anxiety can hijack the present in many ways. Some people are constantly listening to music or to a podcast. Kids waiting for the school bus no longer even attempt to initiate awkward conversations; instead, they all look at their phones. Commuters drive to work listening to their Spotify playlist or a podcast. Couples have a romantic dinner at an expensive restaurant, and instead of gazing into each other's eyes, they gaze at their phones. During the COVID-19 pandemic, sales of alcohol increased as many people chose to have a glass of wine or a cocktail to calm their anxiety.

Some people manage their anxiety by becoming extremely rigid in their behavior and their opinions. They simply will not hear another viewpoint and become intensely angry when someone dares to question their position—this seems to be an increasing phenomenon in our society today as we become more and more polarized in our opinions. But how much of the "my way or the highway" attitude is actually a way of managing the anxiety of facing our uncertain world?

Some triathletes and "gym rats" will confess that they spend more hours exercising than is truly necessary to maintain fitness—but the hours spent running or biking or working out at the gym calm them, keep their fears at bay. When we take that first sip of wine after a stressful day at work, or inhale that first puff of a cigarette, or find ourselves sighing as we take that first bite of heavenly chocolate cake, or pushing ourselves to the limits in search of the elusive "runner's high," while managing to perfection all the details and binge-watching our favorite Netflix show, we are, perhaps, somewhere else for a time: in a land where all is right with the world, in an imaginary land with no anxiety.

It's a bit like taking the batteries out of your smoke detector so you don't hear the alarm. For a while, the quiet is peaceful. But now we're endangering our lives in the event of an actual crisis. The alarm sounds for a reason, and we don't actually want to disable it. The problem is that, with a history of trauma, or even by continually responding to our amygdala, we've created a super-sensitive alarm that goes off too frequently, when we're not in mortal danger — as we discussed earlier. The best approach is not to take the batteries out or disable it entirely. At the same time, though, we don't want an overly sensitive alarm that constantly warns us of imaginary dangers. The best response is to work *with* the amygdala, to *train* it to respond properly and appropriately: to warn us of true impending danger, but not to keep us awash in anxiety.

But how do we train our amygdala? What would it look like to be fully present to ourselves and others, without alarm bells sounding unnecessarily or anxiety making us want to fight or to flee (whether physically or emotionally, through one of our coping strategies)? Where can we find this presence of mind, calmness of spirit, and firm confidence that, with God's grace, we can face any trial?

Chapter 8

When Anxiety Hijacks Our Relationship with God

Martha, Martha, you are anxious and troubled about many things; one thing is needful. Mary has chosen the good portion, which shall not be taken away from her.

—Luke 10:41–42

Saint Francis de Sales used to say that "a truly obedient soul has never been lost"; and that we should be satisfied to know from our confessor that we are going on well in the way of God, without seeking further certainty of it.

—St. Alphonsus de Liguori[126]

Hope comes to assure us on the part of infinite mercy of both the pardon of our sins and the grace necessary to live a good—and even more—a holy life.

—Fr. Gabriel of St. Mary Magdalen, O.C.D.[127]

---

[126] Alphonsus de Liguori, Sermon XXV, Fourth Sunday after Easter, "On Obedience to Your Confessor," *The Saint Alphonsus de Liguori Collection* (London: Catholic Way Publishing, 2016), loc. 10528.

[127] Fr. Gabriel of St. Mary Magdalen, O.C.D., *Divine Intimacy: Meditations on the Interior Life for Every Day of the Liturgical Year* (London: Baronius Press, 2021), 714.

NED: FROM ANXIETY TO SCRUPULOSITY

As a child, Ned was quiet and rather introverted; he grew up in a military family that frequently moved, and he routinely had to make new friends and adjust to new schools. He seemed to handle this fairly well, though in any case, there was no choice about it, and his father was of the mindset that you just "take what you get and you don't complain." At times during his childhood, for example, immediately following a move, Ned experienced anxiety—though he didn't know it as such, evidenced by performing little rituals such as avoiding cracks (he once heard the childhood chant "step on a crack and break your mother's back," and he found it hard to get it out of his mind), counting steps, and being perfectionistic about his schoolwork. In high school, his anxiety increased until, at one point in junior year, he developed mental rituals: counting steps, counting ceiling tiles, and needing to repeat phrases until they felt "just right." This peaked during final exams, but it tapered off when summer came.

Things changed when Ned left home to attend college and found a thriving, active Catholic campus ministry. He had been baptized Catholic, but his family had not been overly religious; they attended Mass regularly but never while traveling, and his religious education was limited to infrequent attendance of CCD classes—if they were even offered at whatever military base he happened to be on. Now, at college, he first became aware of his Catholic Faith as more than simply attending Mass on Sundays. He began making solid Catholic friends who got together weekly to read the Bible and who challenged each other to grow in their Faith. He began attending daily Mass and going regularly to Confession. He even found a spiritual director.

But slowly his zeal for his faith began to morph into anxiety. He worried about sins he had committed in high school: Had he confessed them? If he had confessed them, had he done so properly, with sufficient contrition? He worried about the Communion fast: Had it been a full hour? Did the lip balm he might have ingested count as breaking a fast? Had he perhaps committed a mortal sin since his last Confession? He brought these questions to his spiritual director, but after a few months of meeting, if anything his symptoms grew worse. Although he attended Mass daily, he now rarely received Communion, always finding a possible serious sin he may have committed holding him back. Even going to Confession right before attending Mass didn't work anymore, as he feared that he may have sinned during Mass: Was he, for example, having impure or blasphemous thoughts? Every Mass became agonizing. Confession brought relief, but it was short-lived. After watching him go for a month without receiving Communion, his spiritual director offered to allow him to receive immediately following Confession in his office. But the long-awaited relief was momentary, and his anxiety returned full force. His spiritual director, suspecting scrupulosity, encouraged him to contact a therapist.

What Is Scrupulosity?

The word *scrupulosity* comes from the Latin noun *scrupulus*, which means a small, sharp stone. In late Middle English, the word meant "troubled by doubts." Some people are said to have a "tender conscience"; this means they have a "true" conscience that is very sensitive to venial sin. If you have a tender conscience, you can be reassured by your confessor or spiritual director as to the state of your soul. In contrast, someone who is scrupulous actually sees sin where there is none. He may be reassured momentarily by his confessor or spiritual director that he has not, in fact, sinned. But then additional questions occur after he goes home and starts worrying all over again—and some of that worry is based in entertaining what-if scenarios. He continues to doubt and question, replaying in his mind the situation in question; he may not even be reassured following absolution, because he fears he may not have confessed properly or with sufficient contrition. The momentary relief after Confession or reassurance seeking is a hallmark of scrupulosity, but it doesn't last. This "reassurance seeking" is a compulsion that *momentarily* alleviates the anxiety. Ironically, the seeking of reassurance actually reinforces the obsessive thought (for example, "Maybe I committed a mortal sin; I'd better go to Confession"). By attempting to relieve the anxiety through Confession, the troubling thought (did I commit a mortal sin?) is actually strengthened. As we have discovered, avoiding anxiety reinforces the amygdala's threat response.

The scrupulous person may see as sinful something that is objectively (or in the eyes of the Church) not sinful—for example, Ned's concern that he might have accidentally ingested some lip balm prior to Communion, thereby committing a sin. Or perhaps this person actually suffers from a phobia, an irrational fear regarding sin. Additionally, these individuals may be making an incorrect judgment that their personal behavior is immoral. Commenting on such circumstances, Dr. Kevin Vost writes,

> When we are scrupulous, we may see sin where there is none, regarding thoughts or actions as sinful that other believers, and even the Church herself, would not consider so. In many cases, we feel we cannot be certain whether or not a particular thought, behavior, or failure to act is actually sinful, so we err on the side of presuming it was sinful. We live in a state of doubt that enhances our anxiety and may lead to assurance-seeking behaviors to help curb our doubts.... In psychiatric terminology, when such repugnant thoughts keep recurring, and we keep ruminating about them and fearing them, they are called *obsessions*. The rituals we perform to reduce the anxiety such thoughts produce are called *compulsions*.[128]

Some people refer to scrupulosity as a "phobia concerning sin." This may actually be the best definition, since the scrupulous person does exhibit signs of a phobia, including severe anxiety, and perhaps even panic attacks, surrounding the possibility of having committed sin — especially when they're hoping to receive Holy Communion or are ruminating about the state of their eternal soul. Vost continues,

---

[128] Kevin Vost, *Scrupulosity: Heal Your Mind, Unbind Your Soul, and Let God Work* (Huntington, IN: Our Sunday Visitor, 2023), 19–20.

In other words, scrupulosity is:

- Seeing sin where there is none; i.e., it exceeds the normal Christian aversion to actual sin. It is frequently seeing mortal sin where there is only venial sin....

- A phobia regarding sin; i.e., a distressing, irrational fear about sin [e.g., that we might commit sin accidentally].

- A judgment of personal behavior as immoral that would be considered blameless by others of the same faith; i.e., a harsh judgment of acts that may not be contrary to the Faith.

- An ethical judgment that inhibits actions; i.e., it may interfere with important responsibilities in life.[129]

SCRUPULOSITY IN THE CONFESSIONAL

Even when Ned was reassured that accidentally ingesting a bit of lip balm would not break the Communion fast, he still remained unsure. Additionally, having once heard that someone might commit a mortal sin if they *think* it's a mortal sin (even if it isn't grave matter), he would begin to fret about having possibly committed a mortal sin since his last Confession. He thought, for example, that he might have had lustful thoughts about someone in one of his classes. He worried that he had done what Jesus condemned: "But I say to you that every one

[129] Ibid., 18.

who looks at a woman lustfully has already committed adultery with her in his heart" (Matt. 5:28).

Ned's spiritual director reminded him that to be considered mortal, which means it destroys charity in our hearts and turns us away from God, the sin has strict criteria that are not so easily met as the scrupulous might believe. His director explained this to him and reminded Ned of the conditions that must be met in order for a sin to be considered mortal. For a sin to be considered mortal, it must meet three conditions: (1) The object must be grave matter, (2) the sin must be committed with full knowledge of what it is, and (3) the person committing it must completely consent to it.

In the case of the lustful thoughts, Ned wasn't sure that he hadn't *completely consented* to them! But despite all the reassurances by his spiritual director, Ned seemed unable to shake his doubts and persistent thoughts about his (potential) sins and immoral conduct. He was briefly relieved of his anxiety when his spiritual director reassured him on a particular point, but then further questions would arise, and Ned would begin to wonder, "What if …?" And then he would begin the agonizing process all over again until he could return the following month to seek further reassurance from his spiritual director.

A scrupulous person has great difficulty distinguishing between a sin and a temptation. As a result, he constantly questions whether he has committed a sin. Preparing for the sacrament of Confession is agonizing for this person, and, when he goes to Confession, he worries whether his Confession was valid. When he recalls his past sins, he worries that he may not have confessed them or, if he did confess them, perhaps he didn't do it properly, or perhaps the priest didn't actually understand what he was saying! If he goes to Communion, he worries that he might have committed yet another sin of sacrilege, even if his spiritual director tells him to receive Communion. He has the *feeling* that something isn't right, and that he is yet again in need of the sacrament of Confession.

Because the doubts and second-guessing endured by the scrupulous person are nothing new and are seemingly never-ending, *Ten Commandments for the Scrupulous* was devised in 1968 by Fr. Don Miller, C.Ss.R., founder of Liguori Publications and Scrupulous Anonymous. It was revised in 1996 by Fr. Thomas M. Santa, C.Ss.R., and again in 2013 for Liguori Publications. The second commandment of the *Ten Commandments for the Scrupulous* states, "You shall confess only sins that are clear and certain."[130]

As Fr. Santa rightly points out, if you are scrupulous, no amount of studying, thinking, or questioning your spiritual director will resolve your doubts. What is needed is to change your behavior. Fr. Santa says specifically that part of this change of behavior needs to be limiting the frequency of going to Confession. Once a month is preferable, or even twice a year, if your spiritual director approves of your going so infrequently. This is recommended specifically to scrupulous persons because, for them, confessing has functionally become a part of a *compulsion* that increases anxiety and their fears, doubts, and irrational thoughts about sin rather than drawing them closer to God. This point is not meant

---

[130] Thomas M. Santa, C.Ss.R., *Ten Commandments for the Scrupulous* (Liguori, MO: Liguori Publications, 2013), https://scrupulousanonymous.org/wp-content/uploads/2015/10/Ten_Commandments_for_the_Scrupulous_2013.pdf.

to deny the efficacy of God's grace, but only to explain the reason a confessor or spiritual director will often recommend less frequent Confession for the scrupulous.

When they do prepare to go to Confession, Fr. Santa advises, "I know you feel bad, but what you feel is not, in itself, a confirmation that what you feel is correct.... Your feeling, although very real, does not confirm anything other than the fact that you have anxiety and stress."[131] With this in mind, it is vitally important for the scrupulous person to learn to differentiate between the "feeling" that he has committed a sin and actually committing a sin.

Following the second commandment previously mentioned, a principle that scrupulous people should scrupulously (pun intended!) stick to is, "You shall not confess doubtful sins in Confession, but only sins that are clear and certain." The scrupulous person needs to understand and trust that you cannot have committed a mortal sin unless you are absolutely *certain* you did so and have given your complete consent. The problem for the scrupulous is that they are never certain with regard to knowledge and consent, and they believe their uncertainty *means* they have sinned. They have a *feeling* that they are sinful. But "I feel so bad" does *not* equal mortal sin.

The founder of Fr. Santa's order, St. Alphonsus Liguori, struggled his entire life with scrupulosity, yet he became a great saint and Doctor of the Church, on top of having been a brilliant lawyer and moral theologian. He was born in 1696 in Naples, Italy. As he was growing up, he was very close to his

---

[131] Thomas M. Santa, C.Ss.R., *Understanding Scrupulosity: Helpful Answers for Those Who Experience Nagging Questions and Doubts* (Liguori, MO: Liguori Publications, 1999), 17.

mother, who perhaps also suffered from scrupulosity. From the time of his youth, he was anxious and fearful about committing sin. As a young man, he used to go from priest to priest in Naples, looking for a different confessor or one who would give him a different answer to his questions in his desire for certainty. As a lawyer, he did not lose a case until one day, during a very prominent case involving the Duke of Tuscany, he discovered that he had failed to take into consideration an important piece of evidence. He admitted upon that discovery that his error had lost the case. At this point, he felt his career was ruined and that God had sent him this trial so that he would amend his ways. While visiting the sick, he had a mystical experience in which he heard a voice saying, "Leave the world and give thyself to me."

From that point on, Alphonsus dedicated himself to tirelessly serving the poor and sick, and he eventually founded the Congregation of the Most Holy Redeemer — today known as the Redemptorists. His biographers say that he drove himself ruthlessly, even to the point of exhaustion and breakdown. Fr. Thomas Santa believes that much of this was due to the severe penances he practiced and possibly also to his scrupulosity, which may have caused sleepless nights, indecision, stomach pains, and other physical ailments.[132] Nonetheless, he was the most wise and gentle of confessors, first to be in the confessional and last to leave, treating each penitent with tender mercy and compassion. It was said that St. Alphonsus made people love going to Confession! Because he knew so well the anxieties of the scrupulous person, his writings contain much wisdom and practical advice for the scrupulous:

[132] Ibid., 219.

All the anxiety of scrupulous persons consists in the fear lest, in what they do, they are not acting with scruple merely, but with real doubt as to the act being simple, and are therefore incurring sin. But the chief thing they ought to consider is this: that he who acts in obedience to a learned and pious confessor, acts not only with no doubt, but with the greatest security that can be had upon earth, on the divine words of Jesus Christ, that he who hears his ministers is as though he heard himself: *He that heareth you heareth Me.*[133]

Decoding Confessional Scrupulosity in Therapy

For our purposes, we understand that scrupulosity, as it relates to anxiety, is typically a subset of obsessive-compulsive disorder (OCD) in which the obsession is religious or moral. According to the DSM-5-TR, "OCD is characterized by the presence of obsessions and/or compulsions. *Obsessions* are recurrent and persistent thoughts, urges or images that are experienced as intrusive and unwanted, whereas compulsions are repetitive behaviors or mental acts that an individual feels driven to perform in response to an obsession or according to rules that must be applied rigidly."[134]

---

[133] Liguori, *Alphonsus de Liguori Collection*, loc. 15449.

[134] American Psychiatric Association, *Diagnostic and Statistical Manual of Mental Disorders, 5th Edition, Text Revision* (Washington, DC: American Psychiatric Association, 2022), 263.

If you are unsure whether you or one of your loved ones needs to consult a therapist regarding OCD, but you think you may be seeing signs of scrupulosity, this quick self-test can be a helpful tool. The Penn Inventory of Scrupulosity is the most widely used questionnaire for identifying the likelihood that an individual is scrupulous—that is, that an individual has OCD with regard to religious matters.

THE PENN INVENTORY OF SCRUPULOSITY (PIOS)-REVISED[135]

Instructions: The following statements refer to experiences that people sometimes have. Please indicate how often you have these experiences using the following key:

0 = never; 1 = almost never; 2 = sometimes;
3 = often; 4 = constantly

_____ 1. I worry that I might have dishonest thoughts

_____ 2. I fear I will act immorally

_____ 3. I feel urges to confess sins over and over again

_____ 4. I worry about Heaven and Hell

_____ 5. Feeling guilty interferes with my ability to enjoy things I would like to enjoy

_____ 6. Immoral thoughts come into my head and I can't get rid of them

---

[135] See Jonathan S. Abramowitz et al., "Religious Obsessions and Compulsions in a Non-clinical Sample: The Penn Inventory of Scrupulosity (PIOS)," *Behavior Research Therapy* 40, no. 7 (2002): 825–838, https://pubmed.ncbi.nlm.nih.gov/12074376/.

____ 7. I am afraid my behavior is unacceptable to God

____ 8. I must try hard to avoid having certain immoral
thoughts

____ 9. I am very worried that things I did may have been
dishonest

____ 10. I am afraid I will disobey God's rules/laws

____ 11. I am afraid of having sexual thoughts

____ 12. I feel guilty about immoral thoughts I have had

____ 13. I worry that God is upset with me

____ 14. I am afraid of having immoral thoughts

____ 15. I am afraid my thoughts are unacceptable to God

The score, which can be anywhere between 0 and 60, simply indicates the severity or less severity (or even the nonexistence) of scrupulosity; there is no number that indicates "you now have scrupulosity." Instead, think of this as a tool that you can use in concert with your therapist or spiritual director to identify problem spots.

Ned eventually came to see Lianna in therapy. After discussing his family history and the history of his childhood anxiety that seemed to have morphed into scrupulosity, Ned hung his head and said, "It's so ironic that if I had just stayed a lukewarm Catholic, none of this would be happening now!" Lianna reassured him, however, explaining that in her experience the anxiety and OCD would likely have found another way to manifest in his life as a college student and that, in fact,

OCD tends to "go after" whatever is considered of high value to the individual experiencing it. If we fear germs, for example, then we'll worry about contracting something that might kill us. For the religious person, as we have seen, OCD might result in fear of damnation or of committing a mortal sin. For Ned, OCD attacked his newfound faith.

Not everyone who is scrupulous will be diagnosed as having OCD.[136] Most mental health professionals say that there is a "continuum" on which we might have a "tender conscience" on one end and diagnosed OCD at the other end. From a Catholic perspective, OCD should be treated therapeutically in concert with one's spiritual director or regular confessor.

Rather than continuing to allow Ned to indulge his fears and anxiety by answering the long list of what-if questions about whether he could worthily receive Holy Communion (remember that what-if worries often add fuel to our anxiety fire), Lianna went with the standard exposure and response prevention (ERP) therapy protocol: She advised Ned that, given he had just gone to Confession, he should receive Communion the next time he attended daily Mass, no matter what his doubts were.

When he returned for the next session, Ned reported back, "I was going to receive Communion, but then I worried I might have had a blasphemous thought during the Consecration!" Despite the fact that Ned had tried to dispel the

---

[136] It is worth noting that religion itself is not a cause of scrupulosity. The International OCD Foundation states that while there have been many religious figures who have suffered from scrupulosity, "there is no evidence that the moral or religious character of scrupulosity sufferers is any different from that of other people." Vost, *Scrupulosity*, 88–89.

thought, it kept coming back, and he concluded that he ought not receive Communion.

The struggle for the scrupulous, as mentioned earlier, is that they have difficulty distinguishing between a temptation and an actual sin. Despite both Lianna's and the spiritual director's reassurances that Ned's *temptations* were not actual *sins*, he couldn't shake the *feeling* that he had perhaps committed a serious sin or the panic that came with this thought.

"What if I had a sexual thought about a woman at Mass? I didn't linger on it … but maybe I did linger on the thought more than I should have! How many seconds would count as lingering? Was that in fact giving in to lustful thoughts and desires? Or was it just a temptation?" Ned would question himself, and then he would not receive Communion due to his uncertainty.

Even though his spiritual director told him to receive nonetheless, and reassured him that he was not guilty of a sin in that instance, Ned was not convinced. "But how does he know what the state of my mind and heart really were?" Ned asked. "He can't actually read into my heart!" These intrusive thoughts, doubts, and scruples about sin, Hell, the state of his soul, and so on were his *obsessions*—the *O* in OCD.

"My spiritual director told me that when I'm consumed by a question, it's my scrupulosity speaking, and not an actual sin. He says that after I confess the sin, I should put it in the past," Ned shared with Lianna. The problem for Ned was that, despite this wise counsel from his spiritual director—and despite the fact that Ned understood him intellectually—he continued to doubt and question and seek further answers, disregarding what his spiritual director told him. Instead of acting in obedience to his spiritual director, Ned was acting on his *feelings* of doubt and anxiety.

It was in therapy that it became clear that a further error on Ned's part was the disobedience itself: He was disobeying his spiritual director. Instead of relying on his wise and prudent advice, Ned continued to obsess over his doubts. St. Alphonsus, however, assures us that obedience to one's confessor or spiritual director is the *cure* for scrupulosity:

> The devil labours at length to make scrupulous persons afraid that they will commit sin if they follow the advice of their confessor. We must be careful to overcome these vain fears. All theologians and spiritual writers commonly teach, that it is our duty to obey the directions of our confessors, and conquer our scruples.... Saint Francis de Sales used to say that "a truly obedient soul has never been lost"; and that we should be satisfied to know from our confessor that we are going on well in the way of God, without seeking further certainty of it.[137]

In his discussion of interior trials in *The Way of Salvation and of Perfection*, St. Alphonsus quotes St. Bernard: "The sovereign remedy for the scrupulous ... is a blind obedience to their confessor." But the scrupulous person may object, continues St. Alphonsus, that their confessor is no St. Bernard! To which all the saints reply, quoting Jesus, "He who hears you hears me" (Luke 10:16).[138]

---

[137] Liguori, "On Obedience to Your Confessor," loc. 10528.

[138] Alphonsus de Liguori, *The Way of Salvation and of Perfection*, in *The Saint Alphonsus de Liguori Collection* (London: Catholic Way Publishing, 2016), loc. 15470.

With these words from St. Alphonsus, St. Bernard, and Holy Scripture in mind, anyone struggling with scrupulosity in the confessional must remember this maxim: Obey your confessor; do not seek further certainty!

Lianna suggests that her scrupulous clients meditate on God's loving care for them, which can especially be seen in particular Scripture passages, as for example in Matthew 10:26–31:

> Have no fear of them; for nothing is covered that will not be revealed, or hidden that will not be known. What I tell you in the dark, utter in the light; and what you hear whispered, proclaim upon the housetops. And do not fear those who kill the body but cannot kill the soul; rather fear him who can destroy both soul and body in hell. Are not two sparrows sold for a penny? And not one of them will fall to the ground without your Father's will. But even the hairs of your head are all numbered. Fear not, therefore; you are of more value than many sparrows.

Additionally, Psalm 145:8 reassures us, "The Lord is gracious and merciful, slow to anger and abounding in steadfast love." And in Psalm 86, we find these words of comfort: "But thou, O Lord, art a God merciful and gracious, slow to anger and abounding in steadfast love and faithfulness" (v. 15).

Lianna also reminds her clients that God is a merciful Father who eagerly wants them to have eternal life. He is not secretly watching and waiting to catch us out on some possible sin, then pouncing on us, saying, "Aha! I caught you! Now you're in for it!" Whenever we turn to Jesus and the Blessed Mother, we can be confident that they will help us in our moments of confusion, doubt, and anxiety. Jesus died to save us, and He doesn't wish for us to be lost. "Now I am no more in the world, but they are in the world, and I am coming to thee. Holy Father, keep them in thy name, which thou hast given me, that they may be one, even as we are one" (John 17:11).

Ned would tell Lianna that he knew intellectually that God was loving and merciful, but when it came to ruminating about possible sins he had committed, his knowledge seemed to vanish, and he felt paralyzed by doubts. This, too, was discussed by St. Alphonsus, who insisted that the scrupulous person must "*act* without restraint" and not remain paralyzed by the state of doubt—despite the conflicting thoughts, questions, and uncertainties that were constantly encroaching. This would mean acting, in a sense, against his own will (and certainly against his strong feelings) but ideally in obedience to whatever his confessor or spiritual director had told him to do.

It's Not Me—It's My OCD

As we conclude this chapter, we return to St. Alphonsus, who writes, "So that when there exists in the scrupulous person the habitual will not to offend God, it is certain ... that while he acts in his doubtfulness *he does not sin*." And further, he writes that scrupulous souls should suffer this cross with resignation and "may commend themselves oftener to the Lord, and put a more entire trust in the divine goodness. Meanwhile let them often have recourse to the most holy Virgin Mary, who is called, and is in truth, the Mother of Mercy, and comforter of the afflicted."[139]

Since the nineteenth century and the time of Sigmund Freud, many treatments have been proposed for OCD. However, for more than fifty years, it was considered virtually untreatable.[140] In 1966, British psychologist Victor Meyer successfully treated two patients with OCD using exposure and response prevention (ERP)—an early forerunner to today's cognitive behavioral therapy (CBT). Exposure and response prevention therapy is today considered to be the "gold standard" for OCD, including for the treatment of scrupulosity.[141] The goal is to train the amygdala to decrease its threat response and thereby diminish the need to practice whatever compulsions were intended to alleviate the anxiety caused by the intrusive, obsessive thoughts (compulsions such as refusing to receive Communion, repeating numerous prayers because they weren't said properly, reconfessing sins that have already been absolved in the confessional, questioning one's spiritual director, making deals with God, etc.). Instead, through ERP, lean into the anxiety rather than trying to dispel it.

This is what we might suggest for Ned. But don't try this at home unless your therapist or spiritual director instructs you to do so!

---

[139] Ibid., loc. 15551, 15575.

[140] National Collaborating Centre for Mental Health, *Obsessive-Compulsive Disorder: Core Interventions in the Treatment of Obsessive-Compulsive Disorder and Body Dysmorphic Disorder* (Leicester, UK: British Psychological Society, 2006), https://www.ncbi.nlm.nih.gov/books/NBK56465/.

[141] Vost, *Scrupulosity*, 117. Dr. Vost also cautions scrupulous people to have a trusted Catholic therapist and spiritual director so that this type of therapy is not applied incorrectly by someone who is ignorant of the Catholic Faith.

Imagine you are attending Mass, and at the moment when the priest and the congregation pray, "Lord, I am not worthy," just before Communion, doubts begin swirling in your mind. You *feel consumed* with shame and anxiety and fear: You may feel that you might have committed a serious sin, and that you shouldn't receive Communion in this state. Your soul is in danger! But rather than alleviating your anxiety with whatever strategy (i.e., compulsion) you may have turned to in the past—for example, giving in to the doubts and not receiving Communion—instead … *lean into the anxiety!* Feel the doubts, feel the anxiety, but *know* it is not sin! *It's not me—it's my OCD!* Get into the Communion line, and turn to face God, who alone can carry you across the abyss of anxiety. Just like the person who is afraid of heights, who decides that he will take that step toward the balcony on the tenth floor, you will begin to train your amygdala that this is not dangerous. Receiving Communion in obedience to your director or confessor—despite your feelings of anxiety—will help decrease the anxiety and scrupulosity in the future. St. Alphonsus de Liguori writes about such a struggle in regard to St. Catherine of Bologna, who was afflicted with scrupulosity. He says that she was afraid to receive Holy Communion; nonetheless, she was obedient to her spiritual director, who told her to receive despite her scruples. One day, Jesus Himself appeared to her and told her to have *courage*, "because by her obedience she gave him great pleasure."[142]

The greatest tragedy is that the devil loves scrupulosity. Every time the devil gets in your head enough that he

---

[142] Alphonsus de Liguori, *The True Spouse of Jesus Christ*, in *The Saint Alphonsus de Liguori Collection* (London: Catholic Way Publishing, 2016), loc. 70612.

successfully keeps you away from being closer to Jesus, he's won a little victory. Don't give him the satisfaction of you needlessly distancing yourself from Jesus. Instead, approach and receive Christ in Communion, grow in virtuous obedience to your spiritual director, and don't let the devil win this round.

Making the move out of the amygdala to the prefrontal cortex—from the emotional, alarmist threat center of the brain to the rational brain—takes *courage*. You *feel* doubtful, anxious, confused, consumed … yet you face your fears and continue to take the action your confessor or spiritual director told you to take. Breathe. Remember what your spiritual director and St. Alphonsus told you: "There is no sin."

It's not me—it's my OCD. Doubts are only temptations, and temptations are not sin. Lean into the anxiety, turn back to face God, and He will lift you across the infinite abyss, just as St. Peter was able to walk on the water—so long as his eyes were fixed on Christ.

Despite those very strong feelings that you should not receive Communion, or that you made a poor Confession, or that your soul is in danger of eternal damnation—persevere! Fortitude is needed to stand firm and to face your fears directly; your will can persevere despite your feelings. The virtue of prudence is needed to accurately assess the present situation, to not continually focus on the past, and to take the proper steps to do the right thing. Jesus wants to give Himself to you as sacramental food—so that you may be united to Him in the sacrament of love.

God wants to be with us, to be close to us—so close that He became one of us. As St. Athanasius, one of the Church Fathers, famously said, "God became man so man might become God."[143] As we grow in friendship with God, partaking in the Holy Eucharist, in which we receive the very Body, Blood, Soul, and Divinity of Jesus, we enter more and more into an intimate union with the Holy Trinity. "No longer do I call you servants, for the servant does not know what his master is doing; but I have called you friends" (John 15:15).

So long as you continue in fear, you cannot allow your soul to fly to meet its beloved, that gentle guest who does not condemn you, but who wishes to unite Himself to you. So long as you continue in fear, you will find everything a torture, burdensome and heavy. But Christ came to take our burdens upon Himself: "Come to me, all who labor and are heavy laden, and I will give you rest" (Matt. 11:28). Christ is not like the Pharisees, who "bind heavy burdens, hard to bear, and lay them on men's shoulders" (Matt. 23:4)—so don't become a Pharisee to yourself! Without love, writes Fr. Jean du Coeur de Jesus d'Elbée, "Everything is painful, everything is tiring, everything is burdensome."[144] Remember, "there is no fear in love, but perfect love casts out fear. For fear has to do with punishment, and he who fears is not perfected in love" (1 John 4:18).

With St. Thérèse, the Little Flower, who some biographers believe suffered from scrupulosity for a time during her brief life, you can turn with confidence and love to God, who will lift you up even if you are too weak and small to fly, upon His own wings—if you but abandon yourself with total confidence to His infinite mercy.

---

[143] Wilfrid Stinissen, O.C.D., *Bread That Is Broken* (San Francisco: Ignatius Press, 2020), 78.

[144] *Magnificat* 26, no. 6 (2024): 376.

TIPS FOR SUCCESS IN COMBATING SCRUPULOSITY

1. Find a spiritual director or regular confessor with whom you can be frank about your scrupulosity. Continue to go to this same person for Confession.

2. Acknowledge that these thoughts are OCD/scrupulous thoughts: *It's not me—it's my OCD.*

3. Remember that the *feeling* you have of doubt, uncertainty, or anxiety about whether or not you have committed a sin is not objective reality. If your confessor tells you that a temptation, a passing thought, or a doubt is not a sin, then you must believe him and submit to his authority. Feeling very badly ≠ sin.

4. Be obedient to your confessor. If he tells you to receive Communion, then do so, knowing that this is God's will.

RECOMMENDED READING

Beattie, Trent. *Scruples and Sainthood: Accepting and Overcoming Scruples with the Help of the Saints.* Fitzwilliam, NH: Loreto Publications, 2011.

Bourne, Edmund. *The Anxiety and Phobia Workbook.* 6th ed. Oakland, CA: New Harbinger Publications, 2015.

Santa, Thomas M. *Understanding Scrupulosity: Helpful Answers for Those Who Experience Nagging Questions and Doubts.* Liguori, MO: Liguori Publications, 1999.

Vost, Kevin. *Scrupulosity: Heal Your Mind, Unbind Your Soul, and Let God Work.* Huntington, IN: Our Sunday Visitor, 2023.

PART THREE

Leaning into Anxiety

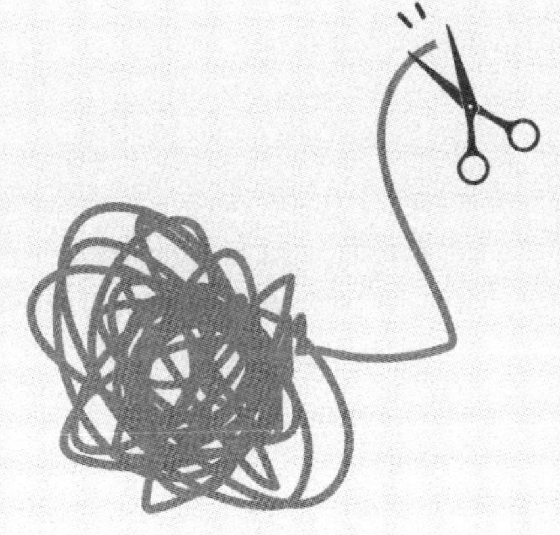

*I saw there was a space I had not
been aware of before.*
—Dr. Russell Kennedy[145]

*Casting all your care upon Him; for He has care
for you. And if it is God who thus gives thought
for our good, why should we weary ourselves with
so many anxieties, as if our happiness depended on
our own cares, and not rather abandon ourselves
into the hands of God, upon whom all depends?*
—St. Alphonsus de Liguori[146]

[145] Russell Kennedy, *Anxiety Rx* (Sioux Falls: Awaken Village Press, 2020), 200.

[146] Alphonsus de Liguori, *The Way of Salvation and of Perfection*, in *The Saint Alphonsus de Liguori Collection* (London: Catholic Way Publishing, 2016), loc. 12234.

*Look at the birds of the air: they neither sow
nor reap nor gather into barns, and yet your
heavenly Father feeds them. Are you not of more
value than they? And which of you by being
anxious can add one cubit to his span of life?*
— Matthew 6:26–27

*For you did not receive the spirit of slavery to fall
back into fear, but you have received the spirit
of sonship. When we cry, "Abba, Father!"*

—Romans 8:15

*Therefore do not be anxious about tomorrow,
for tomorrow will be anxious for itself. Let the
day's own trouble be sufficient for the day.*

—Matthew 6:34

Chapter 9

Mindfulness and the Sacrament of the Present Moment

*Sacrament of the present moment! thou
givest God under as lowly a form as
the manger, the hay, or the straw.*

—Jean-Pierre de Caussade[147]

*If we were attentive and watchful God would
continually reveal Himself to us, and we
should see His divine action in everything
that happened to us, and rejoice in it.*

—Jean-Pierre de Caussade[148]

Karen and her husband, Clem, began seeing Art for marriage therapy. As a couple, they found themselves stuck in a seemingly endless round of conflicts they couldn't resolve. Even a somewhat trivial debate would sometimes upset Karen so much that to prevent herself from screaming at Clem, she had resorted to stomping off in high dudgeon, muttering angrily under her breath

---

[147] Jean-Pierre de Caussade, *Abandonment to Divine Providence*, trans. E. J. Strickland (Overland Park, KS: Digireads Publishing, 2018), loc. 213.

[148] Ibid., loc. 451.

... and then refusing to speak to him for several days. Karen's reaction of—literal—fight or flight was a result of her intense experience of anxiety around marital conflict. Both realized that not only was this pattern hurting their marriage, but also their children were beginning to suffer.

Art acknowledged that Karen's desire to avoid screaming was good; nonetheless, refusing to communicate for days is stonewalling,[149] which only makes things worse. In this extremely common scenario that many couples will recognize from their own experience, a pattern of conflict becomes entrenched surrounding a repeated request to do or to refrain from doing something, which is then repeatedly ignored by the spouse. When intense anxiety arises, when you have that sense that you're "overreacting" to something objectively minor, it is often indicative of a past wound. We're focusing here, however, not on the past wound (also a fruitful topic for therapy) but rather on the *anxiety* itself. Art proposed working with Karen to reduce her intense anxiety around arguments. After all, in marriage there will be trouble, to paraphrase Jesus (see John 16:33). The key is learning how to address conflict in a rational, loving way.

They discovered that Karen had several flash points for intense anxiety. These flash points were almost always related to something her husband would do habitually, causing repeated conflict and sometimes major blowups. Karen was

---

[149] Dr. John Gottman, prominent marriage researcher and founder of the Gottman Institute, found that stonewalling, when it becomes entrenched, is extremely damaging to marriages. Stonewalling is when one partner shuts down (due to feeling overwhelmed by the conflict) and withdraws from interaction with their spouse, essentially creating a wall between them.

waiting for *her husband* to change, for him to do what *she* wanted him to do, or to behave in the way *she* wanted him to behave. Once those things happened, she told herself on some level, then she wouldn't need to explode in rage. But that day never came. So Karen was often either enraged or fuming silently—in other words, she was frequently in *threat* mode: fighting or fleeing.

"Tell me when you experience the most anxiety—what are the triggers?" asked Art.

Karen listed several triggering situations, but Art suggested they focus on just one. She considered, then brought up the fact that, though her husband would offer to help put dishes away, he put everything in the wrong place. "I know I should be appreciative that he even tries to help in the kitchen at all, but why can't he even know where things go? We've lived in the same house for more than a decade! And it's so obvious: utensils in the utensil drawer! Or coffee mugs in the cupboard—where *all* the other mugs are. Is he blind or something?" It was clear that Karen was beginning to get angry just talking about it. "I can never find anything in the kitchen after he 'helps.' And then he gets so angry when I point this out to him. He says, 'I don't know why I bother to help out at all, the way you're so ungrateful!'"

"Hold on to that feeling and stay with it for just a moment," said Art. He paused, then went on, "Now I want you to picture yourself just entering the kitchen after your husband has put things away; notice all the details. Can you picture it vividly?"

Karen said that she could perfectly visualize the space: the utensils in the wrong drawer, the coffee mugs on the counter instead of in a cupboard, and dishes precariously stacked with the largest on top and smallest underneath.

After giving her some time to get the picture in her head, Art asked her, "Are you feeling upset, angry, or anxious?"

"Yes!"

"Where exactly in your body do you feel this anxiety?"

"I'm going to have to redo everything! Only now, all the dishes are scattered randomly all over the kitchen. I might as well have put them away myself!" she fumed.

"Okay, that's what you're *thinking*. But can you pause and try to notice *where in your body* you feel the anxiety and frustration?" Art asked again.

"I feel it mostly in my chest. My heart is racing, and my head feels like it's going to explode."

"Focus on your chest for now," said Art. "Remember how we practiced breathing earlier? Take a deep long breath through your nose, hold it in for a few seconds, and then do a long slow exhale. Try to breathe in that feeling of alarm, hold it, and then breathe it out."

Karen breathed.

"How are you feeling now?" asked Art.

"About the same," she replied.

"Keep focusing on it, breathing slowly, and accepting it." He waited a minute, then asked her again, "How do you feel now?"

"I feel less upset. I think I feel … more calm."

"Do you still feel it in your chest?" Art asked.

"Yes, but it's much less painful now."

When Karen paid close attention to the present moment, allowing herself to notice her feelings instead of venting about what went wrong, her anxiety became less overwhelming and she became more capable of engaging in constructive marital dialogue.

Unpacking the Experience of Anxiety

Neuroscientists examined the experience of anxiety and discovered something fascinating: When we attend very carefully to the present moment, what we're experiencing is not anxiety per se, but rather the *alarm* in our bodies. Our minds place the label of "anxiety" on the experience of alarm. It is the *alarm* in our bodies that elevates the heart rate, quickens the breathing, and readies the body to fight, flee, or freeze. The trigger may be any number of things: peering over the edge of a balcony of a tall building, getting ready to make a presentation to the boss, walking into a room filled with strangers, recalling a traumatic event, or even thinking about driving on the highway. In Karen's case, the trigger was marital conflict—or even simply recalling a particular argument. The trigger can be external or internal, an actual threat or a remembered one. The alarm itself is in our body. We label this experience "anxiety."

But when we're fully attentive to the present moment, we can perceive the *alarm* itself. Usually, we're bent on eliminating the trigger to avoid the anxiety that accompanies it. We retreat in haste from the balcony, we avoid giving a presentation at work, we withdraw in sullen silence when our spouse hurls angry words, we decline the invitation to attend a party filled with strangers, we make an "escape plan," we take the lengthy "scenic" route to avoid highways, we rehash our day trying to analyze where we went wrong or what we should have said—or perhaps we just go shopping or turn on the TV and binge-watch a show. And, as we now know, avoidance only makes the alarm sound more dramatically the next time we find ourselves facing one of those triggering situations. If, however, we were to train ourselves to become *acutely* aware of the alarm in our body *when* it's sounding, what would happen?

DISCOVERING AN EMPTY SPACE

Dr. Russell Kennedy, who suffered from crippling anxiety for decades, discovered something unusual when he first became aware of the alarm in his body. When he sat with the sensation of the alarm itself, he found that, though it was uncomfortable, it didn't spiral out of control. When he began to worry about it, the alarm increased. But when he allowed the sensation of alarm to just be, he noticed something he had never noticed before. "I saw there was a space I had not been aware of before—a spot where I could be with the pain of the alarm but not automatically and compulsively fill the perceived blank with an explanation."[150] The empty space had hitherto been filled with a "snowstorm" of worries. Instead of running away from the trigger or overlaying the experience with his usual coping strategies or defenses, explanations or worries, he now let that space remain empty.[151]

When we're *attentive* to the present moment (fully present to it, without distractions or running away from it) and when we also *accept* the moment as it is (without hating it, becoming angry or frustrated or anxious), we are said to be practicing *mindfulness*.

---

[150] Russell Kennedy, *Anxiety Rx* (Sioux Falls: Awaken Village Press, 2020), 200.
[151] Ibid., 200–201.

Some Catholic readers might object: Isn't mindfulness a practice in yoga and Eastern meditation? Indeed, mindfulness is practiced in both Eastern and Christian meditation, but it is not *the same as* meditation or prayer. Mindfulness is simply being aware of the present moment—an ability to be attentive that can be helpful in prayer and, as we shall soon discover, to reduce anxiety. And as Bishop Erik Varden writes, "To be aware … is not simply to notice what goes on around us, but to display a capacity for sympathetic interest."[152] This sympathetic interest can help us move from anxiety to peace in the present moment.

The use of mindfulness as a *clinical intervention* has been well established by many years of research. It has been proven to help reduce negative thought patterns, diminish anxiety, aid in emotional regulation, and improve psychological health and sense of well-being.[153]

For our purposes here, and to avoid confusion, we are using the term *mindfulness* to mean *paying attention in a particular way: on purpose, in the present moment, and nonjudgmentally.*[154] There are two aspects to mindfulness: attention to the present and an attitude of openness, acceptance, and curiosity.[155]

---

[152] Erik Varden, *The Shattering of Loneliness: On Christian Remembrance* (London: Bloomsbury Continuum, 2018), 132.

[153] Shian-Ling Keng et al., "Effects of Mindfulness on Psychological Health: A Review of Empirical Studies," *Clinical Psychology Review* 31, no. 6 (2011): 1041–1056, https://doi.org/10.1016/j.cpr.2011.04.006.

[154] Ibid.

[155] Interestingly, studies have found that people who score high on "trait" mindfulness (having the ability to be mindful) tend to find it easier to let go of negative thoughts about themselves, have less fear of their own emotions, and tend to ruminate less. Ibid.

PRACTICING MINDFULNESS LIKE IT'S 1599, OR IS YOUR SOUL "IN YOUR HAND"?

St. Francis de Sales, bishop and Doctor of the Church, was born in 1567 and became widely known for his profound yet eminently practical spiritual advice. In his *Introduction to the Devout Life*, he tells us, "Examine yourself often, at least night and morning, as to whether your soul is 'in your hand'; or whether it has been wrested thence by any passionate or anxious emotion."[156] When we are being mindful, as defined earlier, with calm attentiveness to the present moment, we are, in a sense, keeping our soul in our hand.

When Dr. Kennedy decided to remain in the presence of the alarm in his body instead of running away from it, he found himself much more calm and peaceful. When we deny, avoid, or run away from the alarm, the trigger, the pain, or the anxiety, we only increase its tormenting hold over us. St. Francis de Sales vividly illustrates this with the example of a bird caught in a net: "Anxiety arises from an unregulated desire to be delivered from any pressing evil, or to obtain some hoped-for good. Nevertheless nothing tends so greatly to enhance the one or retard the other as over-eagerness and anxiety. Birds that are captured in nets and snares become inextricably entangled therein, because they flutter and struggle so much. Therefore, whensoever you urgently desire to be delivered from any evil, or to attain some good thing, strive above all else to keep a calm, restful spirit—steady your judgment and will, and then go quietly and easily after your object."[157]

---

[156] Francis de Sales, *Introduction to the Devout Life* (London: Rivington, 1876; Veritatis Splendor Publications, 2012), 200.
[157] Ibid., 199.

By running from the perceived evil, you inadvertently reinforce the amygdala's view that this is, indeed, a big threat. When Dr. Kennedy allowed himself to simply breathe through his sense of alarm, he felt peace and a sense of control that he had never felt before. He realized that he could lessen that sense of alarm by stopping what was actually making it worse. And what was making it worse? The worrying, explaining, complaining, and avoiding. "When you feel [the] alarm, make a conscious intention of inhaling the pain. That's right, as much as this sounds counter-intuitive, I want you to focus deeply on savouring and relishing the pain as you breathe in.… The truth is, I am feeling the pain — so why deny it or run from it?"[158] This is acceptance: acknowledging the pain and discomfort quietly and calmly.

How Mindfulness Can Lead to Peace in the Present Moment

In our quest for interior peace amid the storms of our emotions, the crises of the world, and the attacks of the devil, what better place to turn than to the present moment! For only in the *present* moment — not the past or future — is God's grace available to us. In the present moment is God's will — His unique will for each of us — and in His will, as Dante said, is our peace. In a sense, the present moment is the only moment that is truly real. The future has not yet happened, and the past cannot be changed. So often what we experience as anxiety is actually our worries about the past or fears about the future. And whenever we let ourselves do that, whenever we're

---

[158] Kennedy, *Anxiety Rx*, 200–201.

obsessing over the past or worrying about the future, not only do we increase our worry, but we also actually deprive ourselves of the present moment. We miss out on what is happening right *now*, both good and bad things. We only add to our suffering when we're filled with regrets about the past and worry about the future. As St. Thérèse put it, "I only suffer for one moment. It is because people think about the past and the future that they become discouraged and despair."[159]

But, you might object, isn't *anxiety* precisely what we find in the present moment? I'm feeling overwhelmed and panicky right *now*, my chest is tightening right *now*, I can barely breathe right *now*—what are you even talking about, experiencing peace in the present moment?!

Remember: That's the amygdala speaking. Fight, flee, or freeze. But must we obey the dictates of the amygdala? When our amygdala is firing and fight-or-flight reactions are activated, we are merely *reacting*—we are not *rationally responding*. Instead of reacting, let's *pause* and calmly experience what's actually happening in the present moment. What is happening right now?

Most of the time the present moment is just fine, maybe even a little boring. It's not terrible. Right here, right now, what's going on around you? Look around. You're reading this book, you're not in a hostage situation, and your house is not burning down. Maybe your kids are a little loud and rambunctious today, but that's hardly a catastrophe. Maybe you're riding on the subway, reading or listening to this on your way to work. Let's take a look around. Is anyone in danger? Is

---

[159] Jacques Philippe, quoting St. Thérèse from the Yellow Notebook in *Interior Freedom* (New Rochelle, NY: Scepter Publishers, 2007), 85.

anything terrible happening? Somebody *could* walk into the subway car and blow us all up. A freak gas explosion *could* incinerate our house. But, actually, nothing is happening *right now in this moment. Why, then, the alarm?*

Say it now: "I am safe." Notice how those words feel in your body. Do they calm you down?

I am safe.

For those of us with anxiety, these words can be a surprise, and we find ourselves responding with a "Yes, but *what if…*!"And each time we do that, we throw ourselves out of the present moment into some potential fear. Discovering the safety of the present moment is discovering calmness in the midst of the storm. It is finding Jesus in the boat. You thought He was just asleep, but actually He was in control the entire time: "But he was in the stern, asleep on the cushion; and they woke him and said to him, 'Teacher, do you not care if we perish?' And he awoke and rebuked the wind, and said to the sea, 'Peace! Be still!' And the wind ceased, and there was a great calm. He said to them, 'Why are you afraid? Have you no faith?'" (Mark 4:38–40). We believe that Christ conquered sin and death, and yet we doubt that He also conquered anxiety!

One hundred and ten years after the death of its author, a book appeared that quickly became a spiritual classic. The letters and notes written by Jesuit Father Jean-Pierre de Caussade to the Visitation nuns to whom he gave spiritual direction were preserved and then published as *Abandonment to Divine Providence*. De Caussade urges us to embrace what he refers to as the "sacrament of the present moment." In the present moment, we find God's perfect will. To hallow God's name, de Caussade writes, is "to know, to worship and to love his adorable will in every moment."[160] And when we realize that God's perfect will is found in every moment, we now understand that "there is nothing trivial about our passing moments, as they enclose the whole kingdom of holiness."[161] Father de Caussade goes even further and urges us to appreciate that if only we were truly attentive to the present moment through the light of faith, we might perceive God's action in every fraction of a second *and the earth would be transformed into paradise*—for "every moment reveals God to us."[162]

Bishop Conley's Story

Bishop James D. Conley of the Diocese of Lincoln, Nebraska, came from a healthy family "raised by loving parents," with many good friends, physical health, and a God-given naturally optimistic temperament. Yet seven years into his service as bishop of the diocese, his vitality, joy, and optimism disappeared. The first thing to go was sleep. Every night, he would rehash the day's events; eventually, his health began to decline, and finally he was diagnosed with PTSD, major depression, anxiety, and tinnitus.[163]

It is helpful for us to reflect on why a good, holy, prayerful man who firmly believed Jesus' words, "Apart from me you can do nothing" (John 15:5), succumbed so thoroughly to the very depths of depression and anxiety. Bishop Conley humbly

---

[160] Jean-Pierre de Caussade, *Abandonment to Divine Providence* (New York: Image Books, 1975), 51.

[161] Ibid., 52.

[162] Ibid., 37.

[163] Bishop James Conley, "A Future with Hope," Diocese of Lincoln, May 2024, https://www.lincolndiocese.org/afuturewithhope.

and prayerfully asked himself this very question, and he discovered that, while he certainly relied on Christ, he also firmly believed the American stereotype of the "self-made man who pulls himself up by the bootstraps and solves every problem himself."[164]

As he took a leave of absence to regain his mental and physical health, he was accompanied by medical doctors, psychiatrists and psychologists, friends, a spiritual director, and a beloved dog. Despite having felt he had "lost everything," he clung to Holy Mass, the Rosary, and the Liturgy of the Hours. He began to understand more fully what Jesus had meant when He said we could do nothing without Him. He realized his radical dependence on Him, and he began to allow Jesus to take on the burdens he thought he should be carrying by himself. It was not simply a matter of saying his prayers and then getting to work. He had to completely surrender his life to Christ.

Many of us struggle with the same "twisted lie" that Bishop Conley discovered was animating him early in his episcopate. We profess God as our Savior, as the source of all goodness and grace, yet we live as though it is all up to us. Conley's breakthrough insight was that Jesus is not "on the sidelines" cheering us on. He is with us every step of the way, every moment of our life. He is not asleep in the boat, nor is He the coxswain calling out, "Pull, pull, pull!" Rather, we are sitting on His lap, and He is rowing.[165] We must

---

[164] Ibid.

[165] The Dominican theological understanding of grace and our participation in that grace illustrated by the boat analogy was described at a recent retreat given by Fr. John Baptist Hoang, O.P., along with his permission to share it with our readers.

surrender to the Lord all of our cares, all of our toil, and all of our duties of the present moment. For each and every moment is a moment in which God is fully present to us — if we are attentive.

BREATHING HELPS US REMAIN CALM IN THE PRESENT MOMENT

We read over and over again in Scripture that breath is healing and even life-giving. Look at these passages, with emphasis added:

- "Then the LORD God formed man of dust from the ground, and *breath*ed into his nostrils the *breath* of life; and man became a living being" (Gen. 2:7).

- "Remember that my life is a *breath*" (Job 7:7).

- "From me proceeds the spirit, and I have made the *breath* of life" (Isa. 57:16).

- "Thus says the Lord GOD to these bones: Behold, I will cause *breath* to enter you, and you shall live" (Ezek. 37:5).

- "[Jesus] sighed deeply in his spirit" (Mark 8:12).

- "And when he had said this, he *breath*ed on them, and said to them, 'Receive the Holy Spirit'" (John 20:22).

We take approximately twenty thousand breaths per day, according to the American Lung Association. Breathing is an autonomic function—something our bodies do without any conscious thought. We breathe when we're asleep and when we're unconscious. When we're under stress or exercising heavily, we breathe more rapidly. When we're calm or asleep, our breathing becomes slower and deeper. Sometimes, when we're anxious, surprised, or shocked, we hold our breath. For example, when he was a toddler, one of Lianna's siblings had a terrifying habit of holding his breath when he was shocked (for example, when he fell down and hurt himself)—even until he would momentarily pass out!

However, unlike other autonomic functions (our blood flowing through our veins, for example), we can also choose to consciously regulate our breath. For centuries, people have practiced breathing techniques to attain peace, to overcome anxiety, and to pray—even monks in the desert of Egypt as early as A.D. 200. Today many studies have connected controlled, deep breathing with stress reduction, and neuroscientists study the brain's responses to breathing techniques.

A study in 2020 of operating room nurses showed that the nurses who practiced breath-training techniques manifested significantly reduced anxiety, blood pressure, and respiratory rate—in addition to better-regulated brain wave activity and increased visual and auditory attentiveness, all of which could combine to suggest a reduced risk of adverse events occurring in operating rooms.[166]

[166] Linlin Xu et al., "Effect of Breathing Meditation Training on Nursing Work Quality, Occurrence Risk of Adverse Events, and Attention Level of Operating Room Nurses," *Alternative Therapies in Health and Medicine* 30, no. 11 (2024): 65–71.

Another study taught patients with chronic obstructive pulmonary disease (COPD) breathing-based walking exercises, and the results showed reduced anxiety and depression in the patients who had practiced the exercises.[167] The 4-7-8 breathing technique (breathe in for four seconds, hold for seven seconds, then exhale for eight seconds) has also been shown to reduce anxiety. A systematic review and meta-analysis showed that breathing exercises have positive physiological effects on the body, specifically in terms of heart rate and blood pressure.[168] Taking a deep, vigorous inhale through the nose until the lungs are full, then adding yet another inhale, and then exhaling until the lungs are empty was suggested by Stanford neuroscientist Andrew Huberman on his popular Instagram account as a "real-time tool" to reduce stress.

When we think of an upsetting experience (whether a real experience from the past or an imagined future possibility), our breathing speeds up, and both heart and breathing rates become irregular. With this in mind, it is not at all surprising that a person with chronic PTSD may have rapid and shallow breathing as well as irregular heart and breath rates. Dr. van der Kolk focused on teaching breathing techniques and on

[167] Feng-Lien Lin et al., "Two-Month Breathing-Based Walking Improves Anxiety, Depression, Dyspnoea and Quality of Life in Chronic Obstructive Pulmonary Disease: A Randomised Controlled Study," *Journal of Clinical Nursing* 28, no. 19–20 (2019): 3632–3640, https://doi.org/10.1111/jocn.14960.

[168] Piyush Garg et al., "Effect of Breathing Exercises on Blood Pressure and Heart Rate: A Systematic Review and Meta-Analysis," *International Journal of Cardiology: Cardiovascular Risk and Prevention* 20 (Dec. 2023): 200232, https://doi.org/10.1016/j.ijcrp.2023.200232.

fostering mindfulness, among other practices, to help encourage those with trauma to feel relaxed and physically safe in their bodies.[169]

As we saw earlier, for both Karen and Dr. Kennedy, breathing through their experience of anxiety helped them remain calmly in the present moment.

AWARENESS OF THE PRESENCE OF GOD AS AN ANTIDOTE TO ANXIETY

Br. Lawrence of the Resurrection was born Nicolas Herman in 1614. As a young man, he fought in the Thirty Years' War alongside the Duke of Lorraine; however, at the age of twenty-one he left the military after being injured and twice escaping death. He entered the Discalced Carmelites in Paris as a lay brother and received the religious name Br. Lawrence of the Resurrection. For fifteen years, he served as the community's cook and sandal maker, and for ten years, he suffered much through anxiety and discouragement and spiritual darkness about whether he would be saved. He finally found peace and immense consolation through his practice of putting himself in the presence of God.

Br. Lawrence's conversations and letters were later collected and became known as the spiritual classic *The Practice of the Presence of God.* In brief, this volume communicates that once Br. Lawrence realized that God loved him and he loved God and would continue to love God — no matter what — from

---

[169] Bessel van der Kolk, *The Body Keeps the Score: Brain, Mind, and Body in the Healing of Trauma* (New York: Penguin Books, 2014), 270–273.

that moment, he stopped worrying. In fact, he said, thinking (i.e., ruminating) almost always spoils things. Instead, he advised, just focus on loving and serving God. In fact, Br. Lawrence was likely not at risk of losing his soul in his initial distress, but rather was much more likely suffering from the anxiety of the great what-if fears.

Br. Lawrence appeals to the image of Jesus asleep in the boat, while the disciples are terrified: "If the vessel of our soul is still tossed with winds and storms, let us awake the Lord who reposes in it, and He will quickly calm the sea."[170] This was Bishop Conley's liberating insight: Christ is *always* near, and He will always shoulder the burden you are facing.

Whenever we take our eyes off Christ, we begin to sink in the mire of anxiety, worries, past recriminations, future uncertainties, self-loathing, despairing thoughts, harsh accusations, and judgments—just as Peter began to sink when he saw the strength of the wind and the violence of the sea: "So Peter got out of the boat and walked on the water and came to Jesus; but when he saw the wind, he was afraid, and beginning to sink he cried out, 'Lord, save me.' Jesus immediately reached out his hand and caught him, saying to him, 'O man of little faith, why did you doubt?'" (Matt. 14:29–31).

In the present moment, God provides every grace we need. Because we are wounded by Original Sin, we are easily swayed by our fears, anxiety, doubts, and even boredom—tempting us to distract ourselves from the very present moment in which God wants to give us His grace and His peace and reveal to us His perfect will. The French

---

[170] Br. Lawrence, *The Practice of the Presence of God* (Floyd, VA: Sublime Books, 2015), loc. 357.

spiritual writer Fr. Jacques Philippe, who writes so beautifully about another Carmelite, St. Thérèse of Lisieux, in his book *The Way of Trust and Love: A Retreat Guided by St. Thérèse*, explains that at the heart of her Little Way is trust. Trust is what we lack when we turn to everything outside of God, whether we are turning to ourselves to save ourselves, turning to an imaginary future, or turning to distractions and coping mechanisms such as money, power, status, control, comfort, achievement, esteem, or worldly goods. Yet, as Jean-Pierre de Caussade reminds us in *Abandonment to Divine Providence*, everything we truly need for the salvation of our souls and for our true happiness is contained in the events of the present moment, in which God reveals His will: "You have nothing to do but love and cherish what each moment brings, considering it as the best possible thing for you and having perfect confidence in God's activities, which cannot do anything but good."[171]

What would it be like to truly embrace this — especially in the face of our worries, fears, and anxiety?

To return to best practices as identified by contemporary therapists and neuroscientists, we should first identify the *intrusive* and unwanted thoughts that accompany our anxiety. Intrusive thoughts are those you "can't help" thinking but that you don't want to be thinking. It might be a thought such as, "I'm going to make a complete fool out of myself during the next presentation!" while you're preparing your PowerPoint slides for a work meeting. For Br. Lawrence of the Resurrection, these intrusive thoughts were, "What if my eternal soul is lost?" For Lianna's client Janice, it was, "I am stupid and

---

[171] Caussade, *Abandonment*, 55.

worthless, so everything I do ends up screwed up." In the middle of the night, Art used to sometimes wake up, and a simple stray thought, such as recalling a client he had seen the day before, would seem to take on a life of its own: He would replay the dialogue and worry that he had not been helpful to his client. He would be tempted to doubt and second-guess himself. The longer he continued to think about the session, the wider awake he would become, until he would realize: "What am I doing thinking about this at three in the morning! Now I won't be alert and productive with my clients *today*! If I keep getting terrible sleep, I'll ruin my health!" Worry becomes ruminating and compounding worries.

So you've got to start by identifying your intrusive thoughts. Once you've done this, and you feel the rising alarm in your body that comes with those thoughts, *accept* them and the alarm, then acknowledge that you can address those thoughts in the morning when you're functioning at full capacity. Lianna sometimes recommends writing them down so you don't have to worry about forgetting to address them in the morning. Often by morning, you'll find that the thoughts no longer bother you.

CURIOSITY ENCOURAGES CALM ACCEPTANCE

Another way to approach the intrusive thoughts—probably not in the middle of the night, but rather during the day—is to become curious about them. We can be curious about *ourselves* in the same way we might be curious when a friend asks for help: in a positive way, rather than judgmentally (that is, with "sympathetic interest").

Saints and spiritual writers have long been suspicious of curiosity, in the sense that we don't want to be overly curious about inappropriate things such as other people's personal lives, and we need to be careful that our curiosity not lead us to immorality or pride. Curiosity—in the sense of an unbridled seeking to know everything—is certainly to be eschewed. And then of course there's the famous adage "Curiosity killed the cat." In fact, curiosity did kill all of us, through Eve's curiosity about the forbidden fruit.[172] So we should be careful about curiosity, especially when our intention in being curious about something is less than virtuous.

Nonetheless, we can employ curiosity in many positive ways: to move us toward empathy and compassion, to put ourselves in a position of growth as opposed to being in "threat mode"—and to take us away from fear and frustration. Curiosity takes us from the problem-solving left brain ("I know why you're frustrated! You don't know how to stick to a budget!") to the intuitive, holistic right brain ("You look upset; would you like to tell me about it?"). Furthermore, it takes humility to be curious. If you're arrogant and prideful and think you have all the answers, you won't be curious or even care about what someone else thinks! Curiosity can also take us from a fixed mindset to a growth mindset.[173] Best of all, curiosity can dispel anxiety.

[172] James Schall, S.J., in his article "On Curiosity" in *The Catholic Thing* (December 15, 2018), recalls author and scholar Stanley Fish saying that Eve was the "mother of curiosity."

[173] To understand growth mindset versus fixed, see Carol Dweck, *Mindset: The New Psychology of Success* (New York: Ballantine Books, 2006). Curiosity leads to better learning: Celeste Kidd and Benjamin Y. Hayden, "The Psychology and Neuroscience

One of Laraine's friends from her parish recently shared that she had been diagnosed with cancer and would soon require surgery. Laraine assured her of her prayers and asked how she was feeling. Her friend replied with a twinkle in her eye, "Oh, I'm actually sort of excited about it! It's going to be robotic surgery and I'm so curious about that!" Laraine's friend had inadvertently employed curiosity as a means to dispel anxiety.

Why would curiosity help in the face of anxiety? Recall that when the amygdala is sounding its alarm, our bodies prepare to fight or to flee. The sympathetic nervous system is activated, and it signals the adrenal glands, which then in turn send adrenaline into the bloodstream. The heart beats faster, sending blood to our extremities and oxygen to our lungs. All this takes place without our being aware of it so that our brains do not even have to think—we just react in a way that best ensures our survival. Our rational brain—that is, our prefrontal cortex—goes offline so that all our resources in our body are dedicated to keeping us alive. This is immensely helpful when a true emergency is occurring. But what if the fire alarm has gone off when there was no fire? When we're constantly on high alert, we're constantly in threat mode. When we isolate the feeling of alarm and actually focus our attention on it, we can actually begin to dilute its effects. Curiosity comes into play here because it is the factor prompting us to wonder what might be going on that the fire alarm gets triggered so easily.

of Curiosity," *Neuron* 88, no. 3 (2015): 449–460, https://doi. org/10.1016/j.neuron.2015.09.010.

Think about the last time you had an argument with your spouse or with another family member. You might have just automatically fallen into an angry response of, "You always leave all your dirty clothes on the bathroom floor!" or "You never look at the budget before you spend money on clothes!" (Or just supply your own example!) Almost without thinking, you fall into your respective positions, each of you reacting automatically with frustration, anger, or withdrawal. This is the amygdala firing and sending you into threat mode. But wait, is there really a fire that threatens your survival? Or is it simply the alarm in your body? Dirty clothes on the floor are an annoying frustration, but not an actual threat to life and limb. Yet, in the moment, we're operating as though we're threatened. Curiosity can take you out of this automatic defensiveness and tit for tat; it slows the runaway train. No longer are you responding from within threat mode (with its corresponding decreased intelligence), but now your prefrontal cortex is back online. Curiosity and a desire to understand, not animosity, will propel the conversation. Curiosity is a one-way ticket out of the runaway train of threat mode and into the gentle breeze of the prefrontal cortex, where harmony and peace can abide.

Curiosity (in this positive sense) is wonder. It's being open to discovery, open to learning, and being calm and intuitive. It is the opposite of operating in threat and survival mode. As psychologist and Holocaust survivor Viktor Frankl said, "Between stimulus and response there is a space. In that space is our power to choose our response. In our response lies our growth and our freedom."[174]

---

[174] Kennedy (quoting Viktor Frankl), *Anxiety Rx*, 69.

Many people naturally wake up in the middle of the night, just as one sleep cycle is ending and another is about to begin. We usually just roll over and fall back asleep, but if we're prone to anxiety, an intrusive thought slips in, and before we know it, we're ruminating and worrying for two hours. Or it may be that we see that *one* difficult co-worker walk into the meeting where we're about to give our presentation. And then we feel our heart racing or our jaw clenching. Or we catch ourselves *beginning* to feel disappointed as our planned day starts taking an unexpected turn, and then we imagine getting absolutely nothing done all day, and the frustration starts rising. Note these pre-anxiety triggers. Some curiosity about them, too, can help prevent them from intensifying into alarm and anxiety itself. If an intrusive thought occurs in the middle of the night, however, we might not want to practice curiosity, since that could cause us to wake up even more; instead, practice acceptance and a simple, calm observance of the thoughts, allowing them to gently float away, like balloons wafting into the sky.

When you learn to welcome the alarm itself, when you no longer fear it or run from it, you actually have a way to address *all* of your individual fears (fear of public speaking, fear of heights, fear of flying, or whatever they may be) because the alarm is always the same (it's in your body). When you actually welcome the alarm, you discover that it is simply adrenaline. And the adrenaline can be used for motivation and for growth. After all, the alarm is in your body; it's part of *you*—so you are welcoming, appreciating, and becoming compassionate toward a part of yourself. "When we stop and create a space between feeling and thought that connects us to the present, we have solid ground to stand on—and with that solid ground, we can go from a fear-based belief system (governed by worry and a focus on the future) to a love-based belief system."[175] Pausing gives us the space to leave the amygdala and take the elevator to the top floor of the brain: the prefrontal cortex. In the words of the prophet Isaiah, "In returning and rest you shall be saved; in quietness and in trust shall be your strength" (Isa. 30:15).

SELF-COMPASSION: A NECESSITY FOR LIVING IN THE PRESENT MOMENT

Russell Kennedy describes how he needed to develop a compassionate connection with himself to stop the cycle of worry and anxiety, just as Lianna's client Janice from chapter 6 had to experience a moment of compassion for her younger self in order to realize that she was not to blame for the abuse she had suffered during her youth. As a child, Kennedy had no one to comfort him or help him feel safe and secure when he was terrified by his father's psychotic episodes and eventual suicide. Because he had never learned how to find a safe and secure space, he struggled constantly with anxiety, worry, and fear—but even more than that, he would disconnect himself from loved ones and even from himself: "The body keeps the score.... It never forgets our old wounds, and at the slightest whiff of a threat from the past, the amygdala jumps into action ... ready to 'protect' us, but with every activation, it grows ever stronger and more ingrained and locks us out of

[175] Ibid., 222.

a connection with ourselves and with others!"[176] As an adult, Kennedy eventually had to learn to give *himself* compassion and to reassure himself that he was safe, just as Lianna's client Janice had to experience compassion for her young child self before she could stop blaming herself for her past trauma and present problems.

Compassion is important not only for our own self (especially if we have a history of self-criticism and shame) but also for others who may be suffering in the same way we are, or for those who need us to be fully present. Compassion is beautiful in that it can take us out of our anxiety—and, in the right circumstances, save the people around us from their anxiety.

Isn't this also what Scripture tells us? "Perfect love casts out fear" (1 John 4:18).

---

[176] Ibid., 208–209, referencing Bessel van der Kolk's *The Body Keeps the Score.*

STEPS TO FINDING CALM IN THE PRESENT MOMENT

1. Take a deep breath. Pause and be still.

2. Notice the anxiety in the present moment.

3. Become curious. Wonder about it: Where is this alarm in your body? Is it in your chest, or perhaps in the solar plexus? What happened just prior that triggered the alarm? Was there an intrusive thought that accompanied the alarm? Observe the thought, without engaging it. See if you can hold it in your body or in your hand.

4. Accept the intrusive thought calmly, including the anxiety that comes with it. Be present to it, and don't try to fix it, engage with it, or argue with it—especially in the middle of the night. Can you imagine the thought floating away into the sky like a balloon?

5. Take a deep breath through your nose— breathing in the feeling of alarm from that place in your body, hold it for a few seconds—and then exhale with a sigh, letting go of the feeling, breathing out the anxiety.

CHAPTER 10

The Eye Is the Window to the Soul — EMDR

For the Eye altering alters all.
—William Blake[177]

The eye is the lamp of the body.
So, if your eye is sound, your
whole body will be full of light.
—Matthew 6:22

EYE MOVEMENT DESENSITIZATION AND REPROCESSING FOR TRAUMA

On a spring day in 1987, Francine Shapiro, a graduate student in psychology at the time, was out walking in a park when she noticed something interesting as her eyes moved from side to side, scanning the path. She later recalled, "I noticed that some disturbing thoughts I was having suddenly disappeared. I also noticed that when I brought these

---

[177] William Blake, "The Mental Traveller," *The Complete Prose and Poetry of William Blake*, rev. ed. (New York: Anchor Books, 1988), https://erdman.blakearchive.org/#485.

thoughts back to mind, they were not as upsetting or as valid as before.... What caught my attention that day was that my disturbing thoughts were disappearing and changing without any conscious effort."[178]

Shapiro decided to test this unusual experience by deliberately making eye movements at the same time as thinking disturbing thoughts and bringing up unpleasant memories, and the same thing happened. She began studying eye movements with volunteers and eventually developed a standard procedure that consistently achieved the alleviation of anxiety, and then she began a controlled study with victims of trauma. This research became the subject of her doctoral dissertation, which was published in the *Journal of Traumatic Stress* in 1989 and has subsequently been the subject of several decades of research. Since her initial study, there have been many additional studies confirming positive therapeutic benefits of the eye movement desensitization — later renamed eye movement desensitization and reprocessing or EMDR — for combat veterans, people suffering from phobias and panic disorders, crime victims and police, sexual assault victims, accident and burn victims, and more.[179]

This relatively new therapeutic method now has an extensive body of research on its effects related to the

[178] Francine Shapiro, *Eye Movement Desensitization and Reprocessing: Basic Principles, Protocols, and Procedures*, 2nd ed. (New York: Guilford Press, 2001), 7.

[179] Ibid., 11–12.

treatment of PTSD.[180] In short, EMDR is well-documented as being highly efficacious in treating PTSD.[181]

EMDR is considered by the Department of Veterans Affairs and the Department of Defense as a "best practice" for treating veterans who are experiencing post-traumatic stress. This opinion is shared by the International Society for Traumatic Stress Studies, the World Health Organization, the U.K. National Institute for Health and Care Excellence (NICE), the Australian National Health and Medical Research Council, the Association of the Scientific Medical Societies in Germany, and other significant healthcare organizations worldwide.[182]

Although EMDR is used to reduce anxiety, that is not its sole function or goal, as Francine Shapiro notes in the second edition of her seminal book, *Eye Movement Desensitization and Reprocessing*. In fact, she writes, if she had to do it over again, "I would rename the approach Reprocessing Therapy"[183] because eye movement is just one form of this bilateral stimulation that she found effective; bilateral tapping or auditory stimulation can also be used. It is also only one component of

[180] Gemma Wilson et al., "The Use of Eye-Movement Desensitization Reprocessing (EMDR) Therapy in Treating Post-Traumatic Stress Disorder: A Systematic Narrative Review," *Frontiers in Psychology* 9 (2018): 923, https://doi.org/10.3389/fpsyg.2018.00923.

[181] Patricia Novo Navarro et al., "25 Years of Eye Movement Desensitization and Reprocessing (EMDR): The EMDR Therapy Protocol, Hypotheses of Its Mechanism of Action and a Systematic Review of Its Efficacy in the Treatment of Post-Traumatic Stress Disorder," *Revista de Psiquiatria y Salud Mental* 11, no. 2 (2018): 101–114, https://doi.org/10.1016/j.rpsm.2015.12.002.

[182] "The Efficacy of EMDR," EMDR Institute, Inc., https://www.emdr.com/efficacy/.

[183] Shapiro, *Eye Movement*, 1.

a complex and comprehensive approach—including cognitive, behavioral, emotional, and systems therapies—the ultimate goal of which is to "help liberate the client from the past into a healthy and productive present."[184] Instead of just focusing on the emotions we experience when we recall stressful or traumatic situations, EMDR allows us to focus on the *memory itself*, changing the way it is stored in the brain ... and thereby changing the emotions associated with it.

Does this all sound like some crunchy California woo-woo? You might well ask, dear reader, how on earth can eye movements, or any side-to-side stimulation, possibly impact our state of anxiety or relieve the anxiety associated with a past trauma? But if we recall an important fact about the anxious brain, it will begin to make sense.

When we experience anxiety—whether remembering or imagining a past event or experiencing anxiety in the present—our brains cannot differentiate between past or present. The brain state is identical. Therefore, if one *imagines* a past trauma, it will be as though one is experiencing it *now*.[185] This gives a trained therapist the opportunity to help the client *reprocess* the event in a new, less-threatening manner—and from a safe perspective. When the event is reprocessed, it can be stored in the brain's memory banks in a new way, a way in which the client can recall the traumatic event in a less-threatening and more comprehensible way. The client can then recall it without *reliving* it. It can be filed away in memory as

<hr>

[184] Ibid., 2.

[185] In fact, this is how exposure therapy (considered the gold standard) for curing phobias works: When an individual simply imagines the poisonous snake or whatever the phobia is, without having to be actually in the presence of a poisonous snake.

a *bad* event. And the memory will be reassociated with new positive cognitions, such as "I did the best I could as a small child" as opposed to "I am worthless." No longer will the traumatic event trigger the intense anxiety that recalling it once did.

As we noted, though, eye movements are only one way of engaging in "bilateral stimulation" of the brain, which allows the client to enter a receptive state in which they can safely call to mind the traumatic event without reexperiencing the trauma as trauma. If the notion of bilateral stimulation sounds a bit crazy, you might not realize that many of us unconsciously do this. Have you ever paced back and forth while thinking about or discussing a serious or difficult topic? This pacing is a form of bilateral stimulation, and it may be helping you process information as you think. Many people find taking a walk in nature to be particularly relieving for stress. Again, walking is a form of bilateral stimulation that involves a rhythmic left-right pattern, not to mention the calming effect of being outdoors.

Bilateral stimulation is relaxing and helps the client feel less threatened (decreased fight-or-flight symptoms), along with producing a distancing effect (with lessened threat response), so the problem seems less imminent and more neutral — welcome effects when we're recalling a traumatic experience. Shapiro describes working with a rape victim who, prior to EMDR therapy, felt intense shame and fear, constantly reexperiencing images from the rape, along with intrusive thoughts such as, "It was my fault." After EMDR, she was able to think about the incident and acknowledge, "I did very well. He was holding a knife at my throat, and I managed to stay alive." After therapy, the intrusive thoughts rarely occurred, and when the client did think about the incident, her physical reactions were more neutral and less disturbing for her.[186]

EMDR does not change *appropriate* emotions or those emotions that serve as an impetus to action.[187] Nor does it remove the actual memory. For example, one of Shapiro's clients was experiencing anxiety about an upcoming inspection of his workplace by a government agency. This anxiety would be appropriate if the client had not yet sufficiently prepared for the inspection or if there was, indeed, something sketchy about his workplace that actually warranted a poor review. If, however, the client was objectively prepared but still suffering from intrusive thoughts, like, "I'm always a failure!" or "I can never get anything right and I'm sure to be fired!" or "I'll never succeed in life," then these intrusive and inappropriate emotions and beliefs could be reprocessed through the use of EMDR therapy. The client revealed subsequently that he tended to believe he would always fail because of an incident in his childhood that was particularly significant—though not "traumatic" per se, it was a disturbing childhood experience that continued to impact his adult life because of the negative core beliefs about himself that he had developed and that continued to feed into his present work situation. It often happens during EMDR therapy that a client will begin by wanting to deal with a particular incident, then will subsequently uncover during the process of therapy a

[186] Shapiro, *Eye Movement*, 2.
[187] Ibid., 191.

specific childhood memory or memories that actually feed into the traumatic response to the particular incident.

EMDR FOR MARIA

Maria, a young woman in her twenties, came in for therapy to Lianna because she kept "falling into" problematic relationships. Despite being raised in a happy, loving Catholic family, she revealed that she got into relationships with men who "used her" and who only wanted a superficial relationship. "Guys just want to hook up and I don't know how to say no! I'm supposed to be a good Catholic ... so then I break up with them and find another guy ... and the same thing happens. I hate myself! I'm stuck!"

In the course of taking a detailed history, Lianna discovered that her client had been adopted in her infancy. She had very loving adoptive parents and a happy childhood overall, but she had no relationship with her birth mother and very little information about her. And she was the only one of her siblings to be adopted. She struggled with boundary issues and a feeling of self-worth, leading to poor choices in relationships with men.

"I've always felt like a bit of a black sheep," she revealed.

Performing well in school was her only way of trying to subconsciously "prove" her place in her family. As long as she was getting good grades, she could keep at bay her darker fears of inadequacy. Once she entered her young adult years, her tendency to "people-please," along with being unable to set appropriate boundaries, led to her inability to say no when dating.

"I feel like if I don't give them what they want, they'll break up with me," Maria explained sadly.

"Don't you think you deserve to be with someone who cares about you and can respect your boundaries?" asked Lianna.

"I guess I just don't believe I deserve that," replied Maria.

"How long have you felt that you don't deserve to be loved?" asked Lianna.

"All my life."

As Lianna came to know Maria better over the next several weeks, it became clear that the adoption itself was a source of self-esteem issues and her sense of not being worthy of love. Lianna suggested that she might consider trying EMDR therapy, as it might help with some of the childhood fears and wounds that were likely bringing about her present feelings of inadequacy and shame. Francis Shapiro explains that it is axiomatic to EMDR therapy that any present dysfunctional reaction (an inappropriate emotional response) that is not drug- or alcohol-induced—for example, an outburst of extreme anger because your boss asked for a report, or, as with Maria, the seeming inability to say "no" to inappropriate men and their manipulations, along with the intense feeling of shame and anxiety—is always the result of a previous experience, though not necessarily from childhood.[188] There also could be a recent event, such as a car accident or a disaster, that may be the immediate source.

In the absence of an obvious recent traumatic event, there are very often childhood experiences that are influencing the present situation and are contributing to the inappropriate

---

[188] Ibid., 190.

emotional response. In this case, Maria, though raised in a loving family, had unresolved questions and fears related to her adoption. From her adoption, a core negative fear developed: "I am unlovable." As we've discussed already, it's not uncommon for children to blame themselves or feel themselves responsible for the bad things that happen to and around them.[189] As a child, she had developed this belief about herself: Her mere existence had "ruined" her biological mother's life, which was the reason she had been placed for adoption. In her childhood brain, this meant that there was something about her that made her fundamentally unlovable. Her child self was not able to process the nuances of the situation, to understand that the responsibility was not on her, that her biological mother placing her for adoption had nothing to do with her worthiness of being loved—in fact her mother may have deeply loved her. But this false belief led to the crisis of manipulative relationships and lack of boundaries. This core negative fear, expressed through the negative statement "I am unworthy of love," was addressed through EMDR therapy, and Maria soon felt she could replace that negative belief with a positive one: "It wasn't my fault; I deserve better; I am worth it." Eventually, she was even able to come to believe the statement "I am worthy and deserving of love."

EMDR FOR SONYA

EMDR was helpful to another person, Sonya, who was repeatedly waking in the middle of the night after a tragic fire completely burned down the home of her children and

---

[189] Ibid., 44.

grandchildren — though thankfully, no one had been harmed. She would wake up at 3 a.m. in a sweaty panic: heart pounding, adrenaline pumping, fearful that her loved ones' lives were in danger. She asked Lianna whether EMDR might be helpful in such a situation.

After taking a history and establishing a safe place (note that it is important to feel safe in the present moment of practicing EMDR so that the traumatic or unpleasant memory can be brought up in a good context), Lianna began the EMDR session.

Sonya started out by sharing the moment where it had all begun for her: "I have this memory of receiving a text from an unknown number, saying 'This is Jane. We are safe but the house burned down.'

"I dismissed this as a scam — like the hoax where if you reply to them, they next ask you to send money to Nigeria," she said ruefully.

"Another text came, and then another. I finally answered when the unknown person called; it was indeed my daughter Jane! And their house had indeed burned down! They had escaped with the babies, with only seconds to spare — they were barefoot in their pajamas, no phones, nothing else. No sooner had they opened the front door to leave than the entire house exploded in a massive fireball! Everything was destroyed. I sometimes wake up in the middle of the night, horrified. I think how they might all have died. And to think I hadn't even believed those text messages! I was thinking to myself, 'I just want to keep working out in the gym.'"

"When you recall that, what comes up for you? Where do you feel it in your body?" asked Lianna.

"I can feel it even now; my chest is tight, and I feel like I'm struggling to breathe. It goes all the way to the pit of my stomach."

"What does it make you believe about yourself?"

"I should have done something. I should have protected them!"

"Now," counseled Lianna, "bring up the image and the words that go with that reaction, and, noticing where you feel it in your body, follow my fingers with your eyes. Just let whatever happens happen. And we will talk at the end of the set. Just tell me what comes up. If you want to stop, raise your hand."

At this point, Lianna had Sonya follow her fingers for a short period, then said, "Okay, let it go and take a deep breath."

She paused, then asked Sonya, "What came up for you?"

"Well, it felt strange following your fingers — at first I was worried that I was doing it wrong!" she said with a nervous laugh. "Then I started remembering what it was like to get the text and how I didn't believe it at first — I thought it was a scam! And then I thought, 'What if they had died and I hadn't believed it?'"

"Okay, go with that thought. Continue to notice what comes up."

They continued to process through the memory, exploring the thoughts, emotions, and sensations that came up. Sonya noticed the way she had felt upon receiving the text, the feeling of dread and horror that she hadn't believed it — "they could have died!" — her feeling that she "should have protected them" when suddenly she remembered a detail: One of the few possessions to survive the fire was an icon of the Blessed Mother, in a spot right at the heart of the blaze. The icon survived without any damage at all. Specifically, it was the Russian Orthodox icon of the *Protecting Veil of the Theotokos*. And then she knew: All along, they had been under Our Lady's protective mantle!

Of *course*, as a mother, Sonya had felt responsible for the safety of her daughter and her family, but ultimately their lives—and all of our lives—are in the hands of God and under the protection of the Blessed Mother. Of course the thought of losing one's loved ones—especially in such a horrific manner—brings terror and dread. But it was truly comforting to know that Our Lady's mantle was covering the young family, to be able to find rest in the sure belief that God not only protects us but loves each one of us, even counting every hair on our heads: "Fear not; you are of more value than many sparrows" (Luke 12:7). In the middle of the night, when Sonya would awaken to the traumatic memories that made things seem bleak and dark, this was certainly a comforting reminder.

EMDR through a Catholic Lens

Though research on EMDR has been thoroughly examined over the past several decades, including in neuro-imaging studies that identify changes in the brain states, it is still not entirely understood *how* it works to mitigate trauma. There are several different proposed mechanisms as to how it actually works. It may be that the eye movements cause similar brain waves as those that occur during slow-wave sleep, during which vivid memories move into, are processed into, long-term memory storage. Another theory is that the increased load to the working memory during EMDR causes a decrease in the traumatic memory's vividness. Perhaps, too, the psychophysiological changes, such as the activation of the parasympathetic system, result in de-arousal. And these are just some of the theories. Because neuro-imaging is increasingly sophisticated, it is likely that *how* EMDR works will eventually be illuminated.[190] In any case, studies definitely show that EMDR can help reestablish control by the prefrontal cortex — control that is lost during the reliving of traumatic events.[191] And with the prefrontal cortex back online, more creative and less reactive or anxious thoughts can surface. A new way of seeing the traumatic event may appear ("I did very well.... I managed to stay alive" or "All along they had been under Our Lady's protective mantle!"). This reframing, which we will discuss at length in the next chapter, is integral to the healing process.

The beauty of this rather unusual therapy is that it relies on the individual's own unique capacity to heal oneself. As Francine Shapiro said, "There is a system inherent in all of us that is physiologically geared to process information to a state of mental health."[192] This sounds rather dry and clinical, but when understood by Catholics, it speaks volumes. What this

[190] Ramon Landin-Romero et al., "How Does Eye Movement Desensitization and Reprocessing Therapy Work? A Systematic Review on Suggested Mechanisms of Action," *Frontiers in Psychology* 9 (2018): 1395, https://doi.org/10.3389/fpsyg.2018.01395.

[191] Marco Pagani et al., "Eye Movement Desensitization and Reprocessing and Slow Wave Sleep: A Putative Mechanism of Action," *Frontiers in Psychology* 8 (2017): 1935. https://doi.org/10.3389/fpsyg.2017.01935.

[192] Shapiro, *Eye*, 15.

means for a Catholic is that God has created us so that, as embodied souls made in His image and likeness, *we have brains possessing the capacity within to heal and restore mental health*! And it is God who has given us this gift.

Just as our bones can knit themselves back together after a fracture, so, too, can our body heal itself from trauma. But to best heal, our bones must be set back into place, which is sometimes a painful process. And when a psychological injury ruptures our sense of self, sometimes the necessary healing involves "reprocessing" the memories in some way so that they become less disturbing and vivid and are accompanied by healthier thoughts and beliefs.

> *For thou didst form my inward parts,*
> *thou didst knit me together in my mother's womb.*
> *I praise thee, for thou art fearful and wonderful.*
> *Wonderful are thy works!*
> *Thou knowest me right well.*
> —Psalm 139:13–14

It is comforting and enlightening to reflect on the fact that God has created us in His image and likeness, and that we are indeed "wonderfully made"—with built-in healing mechanisms for body and mind. As Catholics, we also know that we have infused in us at Baptism the supernatural virtue of hope; and Jesus said, "Ask, and it will be given you; seek, and you will find; knock, and it will be opened to you" (Matt. 7:7).

This is remarkable, and it is such a beautiful detail of God's goodness—a detail that gives all of us hope! It gives us hope that we can overcome a history of trauma, abuse, "dysfunctional residue from the past," and anxiety. Indeed, in hope we are saved. With the grace of God, a trained therapist, and our own body's ability to heal itself, we can say, with the Psalmist, "Out of my distress I called on the LORD; the LORD answered me and set me free. With the LORD on my side I do not fear" (Ps. 118:5–6).

We have included these illustrations of EMDR therapy as one specific type of therapy that has been thoroughly studied and well-documented as a means to help individuals heal from trauma — a treatment technique that Lianna, as EMDRIA trained, uses in conjunction with her individual therapy. Nonetheless, there are many other highly effective therapies for dealing with trauma and anxiety that we're not able to address in this book, such as cognitive behavioral therapy (CBT), cognitive processing therapy (CPT), internal family systems (IFS), emotion-focused therapy (EFT), and others. But perhaps even more significant than an effective model of healing — of which there are many — is a good relationship with a trusted therapist with whom you feel confident and safe. Anxiety and trauma, by their nature, are isolating and restrictive of interpersonal growth. Strong relationships — both within the context of therapy and without — are integral to healing and growth. As human persons created in the image and likeness of God — a communion of Divine Persons — we are, by nature, interpersonal beings who draw strength, healing, and transformation from our strong, healthy relationships, the most important of which is our relationship with our Creator.

Chapter 11

Reframing: A Different Frame of Mind Makes All the Difference

The field of anxiety is situated as something framed.
—Jacques Lacan[193]

Anxiety is simply adrenaline with a negative frame.
—Kevin Majeres, M.D.[194]

Do you believe that I am able to do this?
—Matthew 9:28

Jesus the Divine Physician

There came a woman of Samaria to draw water. Jesus said to her, "Give me a drink." For his disciples had gone away into the city to buy food. The Samaritan woman said to him, "How is it that you, a Jew, ask a drink of me, a woman of Samaria?" For Jews have no dealings with

---

[193] Jacques Lacan, *Anxiety: The Seminar of Jacques Lacan, Book X*, ed. Jacques-Alain Miller (Cambridge: Polity Press, 2014), 75.

[194] Kevin Majeres and Sharif Younes, "Challenging Anxiety," *The OptimalWork Podcast*, episode 106, https://optimalwork.com/the-podcast.

Samaritans. Jesus answered her, "If you knew the gift of God, and who it is that is saying to you, 'Give me a drink,' you would have asked him, and he would have given you living water." The woman said to him, "Sir, you have nothing to draw with, and the well is deep; where do you get that living water? Are you greater than our father Jacob, who gave us the well, and drank from it himself, and his sons, and his cattle?" Jesus said to her, "Every one who drinks of this water will thirst again, but whoever drinks of the water that I shall give him will never thirst; the water that I shall give him will become in him a spring of water welling up to eternal life." The woman said to him, "Sir, give me this water, that I may not thirst, nor come here to draw." (John 4:7–15)

Countless theologians, Scripture scholars, and saints have commented on and analyzed this passage of the Samaritan woman at Jacob's well in the Gospel of John. But we're going to take a somewhat different approach from most of these commentators in understanding what is going on here. When we read this, we see Jesus accomplishing a rather remarkable psychological strategy. He draws the woman from her natural desire and need for water to a supernatural understanding of her even more significant desire and need for the life-giving waters of eternal salvation.

Jesus seems to be employing a strategy we therapists would call reframing. The Samaritan woman had come to the well in the heat of the day, unlike the other women of the town who would come in the cool of the morning. She comes at this time of day because she is avoiding women who likely look down on her for having had several husbands and even now living with another man. Jesus reframes the negative situation into a positive one: "Every one who drinks of this water will be thirsty again, but those who drink of the water that I will give them will never be thirsty." He reframes a mundane need for water—a daily task performed in the heat of the day to avoid being scorned or derided—as a deeper, more profound yearning for eternal life. Jesus takes her through a simple reframe to a place that is true, noble, and good—inspiring hope and charity in her and ultimately transforming her: "Many Samaritans from that city believed in him because of the woman's testimony" (John 4:39). This psychological strategy can have a profound impact on our frame of mind, our perspective, and ultimately our emotional and spiritual health.

How do we define this strategy? Reframing is thinking about a situation (often a negative one) in a different, positive, or alternative light. It is often used in therapy, especially cognitive therapy. Reframing is intentionally looking at a particular event or stimuli from a new perspective. To take a simple example, let's say I'm stuck in slow, bumper-to-bumper traffic on a daily commute. My usual reaction is irritation, impatience, and the temptation to look at my cell phone to relieve the stress and boredom. This time, however, I decide to reframe the situation. I pause, and I say to myself, "Here is a perfect opportunity to practice patience. I know that this is typically hard for me, but I'll try to calmly relax for the next minute or two and chalk it up to an opportunity to grow in this critical virtue."

I challenge myself not only to *see* it a particular way but also to *experience* it differently. The new perspective and experience help me to respond in a new and different way rather than continuing to react in an automatic or historically typical way. Let's take another example, where anxiety and emotions were high and where reframing became crucial.

LARAINE LEARNS TO REFRAME

One day, Laraine and Lianna were taking a rather long drive to pick up a unique piece of furniture Lianna had found on Facebook Marketplace. Laraine took the opportunity to share with Lianna a frustrating situation at work. Laraine believed her immediate supervisor was hypercritical of those who reported to her, and was especially sharp whenever she herself felt stressed or overwhelmed by her managerial responsibilities. When Laraine's boss would correct or criticize her work, Laraine felt she was hinting that she was performing at a subpar level. Unfortunately, this caused Laraine to go into threat mode and to react either by angrily arguing with her boss or dramatically stomping off, which prompted her supervisor to comment that Laraine was being "overly emotional." It seemed she could do nothing right from her boss's perspective. She told Lianna, "Just yesterday I was so angry, so upset, that I almost just quit on the spot. And I'm seriously thinking about it!"

"But do you have any other employment opportunities immediately available?" asked Lianna cautiously.

"No, but I can't stand this anymore. It's a daily emotional roller coaster! And I think she secretly wants to fire me."

"But if that's true, and you quit, wouldn't you be playing right into her hands?"

"Well … I guess so."

"And besides, do you want her to be in charge of your own employment decisions? By getting so upset with her that you want to quit, you're essentially allowing her to dictate not only your emotions—but potentially your future job."

"I guess you have a point," Laraine allowed.

"Should this woman be in charge of your emotional health *and* your life decisions?"

"No. I just never really thought of it that way."

Laraine suddenly saw things from a different perspective—perhaps a more realistic one—and she realized that she was giving her boss way too much control over her own life. In fact, our happiness does not depend on anything outside of us. Happiness is an inside job, as the famous expression goes. Nor should important life decisions such as leaving gainful employment be made simply out of an angry or emotional reaction in the heat of the moment. How many times have we blamed someone else for causing us to react in a certain way? In fact, nobody can *cause* us to be happy or sad or angry. That's our choice. We can react according to our own immediate inclinations, or we can more calmly respond in a prudent, rational manner. Laraine knew this on an intellectual level. However, under pressure, she had reverted to an emotional reaction that was temperamentally instead of rationally based. She had not stopped to reflect on whether or not her reaction was actually the most prudent response, and of course it wasn't. Pausing to reflect and taking time to view the situation from a different angle allowed her to reframe it in a more positive, self-empowering light. She saw the opportunity for growth rather than simply reacting in a knee-jerk (and ultimately self-hindering) fashion.

The reframe was this: Your boss (no matter how annoying, despicable, or horrendous she may *seem to be*) does not control your emotional life, nor does she make your decisions for you. *You are in charge* of your emotions; you may choose to react emotionally with anger, tears, and anxiety, or you can choose to respond more thoughtfully, with tolerance and equanimity. *You are in charge* of your life decisions. You can choose to quit in a huff and in the middle of an emotional outburst, or you can rationally and prudently choose to stay in your job—despite some difficulties and challenges that you may or may not be able to sort out—until the time that *you prudently and rationally choose* to leave. You can choose to play the long game.

The immediate—and, frankly, surprising—benefit of this new strategy, however, as Laraine later told Lianna, was that she felt a huge sense of relief, and no more anxiety. She felt relief that she didn't have to rehearse in her mind arguments between her and her boss, relief that she didn't need to wake in the middle of the night with self-recriminations about the way she had handled a particular situation, relief that she didn't have to immediately start looking for employment, relief that she didn't have to face tense and stressful interchanges every day. She realized it was in her power to change her own attitude and quality of interactions between herself and her boss.

And this is the crucial shift enabled by the reframe: Laraine went from being in "threat mode"—amygdala firing, ready to *literally* fight or flee, anxiety symptoms flaring, executive brain function going offline—to "growth mode." In growth mode, she experienced a sense of calm, the executive function of her brain came back online, and she could then make thoughtful and rational decisions.

As a rather surprising result of this reframing, Laraine began to get along much better with her boss. Once she wasn't always reacting emotionally and defensively to her superior's directives, her boss in turn could relax while giving assignments instead of walking on eggshells around her somewhat temperamental employee. She didn't need to aggressively assert her position of authority, since Laraine was now behaving with appropriate deference to her boss. And, with her new-found ability to simply accept her boss's personality with all its quirks, Laraine became better able to *work through* the challenging situations *for the sake* of her goal to leave the employment on her own terms, rather than being "forced into" quitting because her anger and emotions got the better of her. She would be able to stay in her present job or leave at the most prudential time, not out of a fit of emotional pique.

This reframe was certainly more challenging than the traffic reframe, but, as with the traffic reframe, it involved the virtue of patience. Patience is a firm commitment to withstand whatever storms (whether external or internal) are buffeting and threatening you. Moreover, Laraine needed to cultivate the cardinal virtues of prudence, temperance, justice, and fortitude. She needed prudence to rationally determine the best means to achieve the right ends; justice to acknowledge that her boss had legitimate authority over her to direct her work; temperance in how she chose to express or not express her feelings; and fortitude to face up to her own fears and to persevere, despite wanting to quit. Often when we react in a knee-jerk fashion, with our emotions running high, we fail to utilize self-control and prudential judgment, and we also fail to see the potential for growth in the face of challenges. Moreover, once we realize the right means necessary to do the right thing—that is, to respond patiently, thoughtfully, and rationally rather than flying off the handle—we're then able to choose the best road ahead.

You Learn to Reframe

This principle can be applied to much more difficult and emotionally fraught situations than the ones we've described—situations where we're strongly tempted to try to change the other person or the circumstances. But rather than changing some outside influence, reframing changes *our* perspective. Instead of changing the world, I change myself. Instead of changing the other person or telling them how they should be or act, I change myself. Jesus tells us emphatically, "You hypocrite, first take the log out of your own eye, and then you will see clearly to take the speck out of your brother's eye" (Matt. 7:5). This doesn't mean putting on rose-colored glasses and pretending life is a bowl of cherries, nor does it mean blaming ourselves for the bad things that happen; rather, it means being brutally realistic about what is ours to control and what is not. We can, in fact, control only ourselves, how we behave, and how we respond. Most of our clients who have tried this technique have actually reported back to us that the reframe is not simply another point of view, but is actually a better point of view—it is reality, both clarifying and inspiring.

Consider this: When we visit the Louvre to view the *Mona Lisa*, we never go with the intention of admiring the frame. Leonardo da Vinci's masterpiece doesn't need a frame. Van Gogh's paintings don't need a frame. Their works stand on their own. So, what is the point of a frame? The frame may actually serve a practical function; in the case of the *Mona Lisa*, the painting is not on canvas but rather on wood, so the frame protects it from becoming warped or damaged by humidity. But, aside from such practical uses, what function might a frame serve? A frame can cue us to be in a certain disposition of mind when approaching a painting. Perhaps it reminds us that there is something special here, or that we should respond aesthetically with an attitude of searching for beauty—rather than viewing the image inside as a mere poster, sign, or advertisement. Indirectly, the frame tells us, "View what is within, do so with an aesthetic eye, and behold the beauty."

And this is the function of the reframe: It offers a new look at a situation we're facing, a new glance with an eye toward seeing the potential beauty, and even the deeper reality, therein. When we see things from this different and better perspective, we shift into a higher brain function, one that can handle calmly solving a problem, responding virtuously with love, and growing—instead of simply fighting or fleeing the situation.

When we commit to healthy spiritual, emotional, and interpersonal growth, we also need to pause and reflect on how our typical "knee-jerk" reactions might not be the most virtuous, loving, or growth enhancing. We must ponder and pause before we respond. Consider what happened when the angel Gabriel informed Zechariah that he would have a son (see Luke 1:11–22). Zechariah did not pause to reflect and ponder in his heart. Instead, he reacted with immediate disbelief. As a result, he was forced to ponder in silence what had happened, until the naming of his son — and until, presumably, he grew in faith and trust in the Lord.

In contrast, when the angel Gabriel announced to Mary, "You will conceive in your womb and bear a son, and you shall call his name Jesus. He will be great, and will be called the Son of the Most High; and the Lord God will give to him the throne of his father David, and he will reign over the house of Jacob for ever; and of his kingdom there will be no end" (Luke 1:31–33), Mary paused and reflected, but she did not doubt. She responded with her fiat: "Behold, I am the handmaid of the Lord; let it be to me according to your word" (Luke 1:38).

Our Catholic Faith gives us ample opportunity to reframe. Think of Jesus' Sermon on the Mount. For the people there listening, He overturned so many long-held beliefs and expectations: "Blessed are the poor in spirit, for theirs is the kingdom of heaven. Blessed are those who mourn, for they will be comforted. Blessed are the meek, for they will inherit the earth," He said, continuing with five more paradigm-shifting statements (see Matt. 5:1–12). Our Lord also teaches us that when we see someone who is hungry, thirsty, naked, a stranger, sick, or in prison, we actually see Jesus Christ Himself (Matt. 25:35–37). Talk about a reframe!

But even more than that, the crucifix itself is perhaps the ultimate reframe: The implement of humiliation, torture, and agonizing death becomes the means of our eternal salvation. Though you might never hear the word *reframing* used in the theology books in this context, our Faith teaches us to see the inevitable ordeals and frustrations of life as opportunities to view things from a new perspective and to grow in love for God and others. Complex Pauline theology was contained in the little pre–Vatican II nugget "Offer it up." We see each small (or large) difficulty or struggle or pain as something we can *offer to God* for the sake of our loved ones, in expiation for our own sins, and for the benefit of the Church. As St. Paul wrote to the Colossians: "Now I rejoice in my sufferings for your sake, and in my flesh I complete what is lacking in Christ's afflictions for the sake of his body, that is, the church" (1:24). Of course, there is much more to this than reframing; it does in fact contain the entire theology of grace and the mystical Body of Christ. But more immediately, we can use it to remind ourselves to "offer it up," and so we can take the first step in a crucial perspective shift.

The reframing frame of mind isn't just putting a different spin on things, and neither is it slapping a surface smiley face on a difficult situation. It is, rather, an ontological acknowledgment of deeper realities than those that are immediately apparent. It is a challenge to see things as they really are—instead of from our own limited and immediate perspectives. Ned (Lianna's scrupulous client) was eventually able to reframe his torturous, obsessive thoughts as, "It's not me—it's my OCD," which is actually true! Just as the Samaritan woman at the well was drawn from a mundane quest for water to a higher reality and deeper desire for salvation, so, too, re-framing in our day-to-day living can bring us to a deeper, more beautiful understanding of our lives as a whole—from the perspective of truth itself. As St. Paul reminds us, "we have the mind of Christ" (1 Cor. 2:16).

Recently, Art was speaking with someone who had been married more than fifty years about his beloved and recently deceased spouse. This man said that one of the great blessings of their marriage existed in the problems they had, some of them very serious. Every problem or challenge they encountered tested their love and required them to redouble their commitment to each other, which in turn strengthened their love and their marriage. This fellow and his wife knew how to reframe a situation—a lifetime's worth of situations.

Cyrano Learns to Reframe

Question: What do Johnny Carson and other shy people fear when they are caught in a "one-on-one" conversation at a cocktail party? That is, what is the worst case, the worst thing that can happen?... That neither of you has anything to say and therefore the world will come to an end, or rather, something worse than the end of the world, or, as Carson would say, panic city—that is, a predicament in which all options open to you are more intolerable than the end of the world?

—Walker Percy[195]

---

[195] Walker Percy, *Lost in the Cosmos: The Last Self-Help Book* (New York: Farrar, Straus & Giroux, 1983), 32.

Art once had a young adult client who was having trouble meeting women. Cyrano would attend various Church events, such as Theology on Tap, which would attract like-minded Catholics. Art agreed this was a good initial strategy, so what was the problem? Cyrano would arrive at the event and, as people would gather into small groups or circles, he found himself standing alone. He couldn't muster the courage or gumption to break into an existing circle or conversation. So instead he would just continue standing alone on the outskirts, feeling increasingly out of place and self-conscious. He would often end up leaving the event concluding that it had been a waste of his time.

"What is it that prevents you from going up to one of the groups of people or joining in one of the conversations?" Art asked. Cyrano feared that doing so might interrupt the conversation and that he would thereby be unwelcome or even rejected. The potential for such an outcome was too painful to allow him to even consider the possibility of entering the groups, so he continued stationing himself on the perimeter, alone.

Together, within the safety of Art's office, far from the madding crowd, Art and his client analyzed the threat. Art pointed out that although it was logically possible that an event for young Catholics to meet one another might attract those who would be rude and unwelcoming to a newcomer, it was more likely that the attendees would be friendly. After all, one of the main goals of such events was for young Catholics to meet one another. Art's client agreed that if he attended one hundred such events, it might be possible that once or twice he would get a cold shoulder, but probably not a "Get out of here!" rejection.

Art's goal in this conversation was to help Cyrano reframe his situation as a potentially positive one. Art wanted to take his client from the amygdala threat center and into his prefrontal cortex, where he could think more rationally and realistically about the event. In fact, Art suggested, a new person entering a preexisting circle might bring about the exact result everyone present was hoping for: the chance to meet new people. Putting it in this light allowed the situation to be reframed from a fear-inducing threat of potential rejection to the result everyone is hoping for.

Reframing is a very low-threat exercise, but it is also a good opportunity to walk ourselves from a scary, dark, and dingy basement up the stairs into a room where the lights are on, the windows are open, and possibilities abound. The change is not so much out there, but in our hearts and minds. We apply a new frame to see the circumstances of a particular situation not as a threat to dread but as a potentially beautiful opportunity to grow.

However, the years of habitually avoiding or dreading such encounters takes its toll. For Cyrano, avoidance had become such an ingrained habit over the years that he was far too comfortable continuing to avoid similar situations. In fact, as we learned in previous chapters, when the amygdala is indulged repeatedly, it actually grows stronger in its alarm. This means that, despite the fact that Cyrano had now rationally allowed for the possibility that he might enter one of the intimidating circles without actual danger, he still had to prepare for the very real occasion when the alarm would be sounding, "Danger! Avoid! Too risky!"

Together, Art and Cyrano discussed what would happen if Cyrano ignored the amygdala and entered into the circle. It would probably be uncomfortable for five or ten minutes, give or take. But both agreed that, other than being uncomfortable or awkward for a short while, there was very little actual danger.

"Do you think you could handle a few minutes of discomfort as a cover charge to enter the circle?" Art asked him. When Cyrano nodded, Art said, "Okay, let's practice it now."

Art asked Cyrano to work on rhythmic, slow breathing to get himself out of threat mode and to become more relaxed. Then he told him to imagine walking over to one of the circles of strangers. Imagining this would help to get his mind in the free air of the prefrontal cortex by seeing such a situation not as an ordeal or a burden but as an opportunity to learn a new skill and to grow. Like most growth opportunities, it would probably be a bit difficult, especially at first, but it would be worth it: a reasonable cover charge.

As Cyrano imagined himself walking into such a circle of unknown young people, Art told him to shut his eyes and asked him to share how he was feeling as he walked up to the circle.

"Nervous," Cyrano said.

"Where in your body do you feel that tension or nervousness?"

As is often the case in situations when anxiety flares up, Cyrano had never really thought about where he felt his discomfort. And the discomfort was, as it often is, right in the middle of his chest. So Art instructed him to focus on that uncomfortable feeling over a short period of time, and eventually Cyrano found it subsiding.

This exercise better prepared him for the real event. Additionally, Art suggested that walking up to the circle of strangers might also be a bit exciting; Cyrano might get an adrenaline rush, which feels similar to anxiety but is not actually the same thing. Remember that we get adrenaline when we do something challenging: It gives us the energy and the mental alertness we will need to meet the forthcoming challenge. It helps us to do our best and to be our best, increasing our clarity and our energy as we walk toward a new and exciting task.

At a subsequent session, Cyrano relayed what had happened as he practiced all he'd learned, from reframing the situation to refusing to let the amygdala's alarm prevent him from entering the circle. Though he had not yet met the love of his life, he had been to two events and had successfully entered several different circles of chatting people. The more he did it, the easier it became. It was not totally trouble-free, but it was definitely easier, and it was not debilitating or even embarrassing. He found the second and third entries easier than the first. Art discussed with Cyrano that he was training his amygdala to see these portals of entry not as threats but merely as awkward transitions. And Art emphasized how courageous his young client was to deliberately and intentionally pay the price of discomfort in order to have the opportunity to grow and to overcome a self-generated fear. What a great feeling, when we don't avoid difficulties but see them as opportunities to grow in virtue! And all the while, the amygdala is paying attention, learning that this once-dreaded situation is really no longer a big deal.

How to Reframe

1. Acknowledge the situation, accept it as it is, and remind yourself that this does not mean we are condemned to repeat it forever. Transformation is possible.

2. Pause before reacting. Take a calming breath. Now you're going to shift gears from the amygdala and threat mode to the prefrontal cortex and growth mode.

3. Widen the lens. We can reframe the situation and bring a new perspective to it. Reframing allows us to respond prudently and rationally. To find this alternative perspective, try asking yourself the following questions:

    ✠ "What would I tell a friend if he or she were in my situation?"

    ✠ "How would Our Lord see this situation?"

    ✠ "What would my mentor advise me in this situation?"

    ✠ "How would I view this from my deathbed?"

In a sense, we're trying to get out of a narrow egocentric position to embrace a larger view—which tends to be not only more positive but also more accurate.

4. Acknowledge the "cover charge"—we have no difficulty acknowledging the cover charge to enter an exclusive club, but there are cover charges inherent in many situations (for example, the feeling of awkwardness as you begin a conversation, or the fact that being gainfully employed means answering to a superior).

CHAPTER 12

The Purifying Furnace of Anxiety

*In hoping, we lift ourselves above the badly
existing. We forgive it, expecting something
altogether other.... To hope means to be
intensely prepared for what is to come.*
—Byung-Chul Han[196]

*Nebuchadnezzar said to them, "Is it true, O
Shadrach, Meshach, and Abednego, that you do not
serve my gods or worship the golden image which I
have set up? Now if you are ready when you hear the
sound of the horn, pipe, lyre, trigon, harp, bagpipe,
and every kind of music, to fall down and worship
the image which I have made, well and good;
but if you do not worship, you shall immediately
be cast into a burning fiery furnace; and who is
the god that will deliver you out of my hands?"*

*Shadrach, Meshach, and Abednego answered the
king, "O Nebuchadnezzar, we have no need to
answer you in this matter. If it be so, our God*

---

[196] Byung-Chul Han, *The Spirit of Hope* (Cambridge: Polity Press,
2024), 27.

> *whom we serve is able to deliver us from the burning fiery furnace; and he will deliver us out of your hand, O king. But if not, be it known to you, O king, that we will not serve your gods or worship the golden image which you have set up."*
>
> —Daniel 3:14–18

What Have We Learned?

There are some who might insist that anxiety is simply a necessary aspect of fallen humanity, of the human condition. And this is, in part, what von Balthasar suggests in his book *The Christian and Anxiety*: There is "sin anxiety" as part of our fallen human nature that is overcome by Christ and that we are admonished to fight against. And we have all experienced a certain anxiety, as struggling members of the Church Militant, that Balthasar calls a "Christian" sort of anxiety[197] when we fail to live up to our baptismal promises and we worry that we are being lukewarm, like those Laodiceans whom Christ will spit from His mouth at the end of time (Rev. 3:16).

Yet the fact that anxiety has been dramatically rising—especially among young people—over the past decade would indicate that something else is also afoot.[198]

Furthermore, the theory that anxiety is simply being more widely reported, as opposed to *actually* increasing, has been disproven, as shown by the dramatic increase in hospitalizations

---

[197] Hans Urs von Balthasar, *The Christian and Anxiety* (San Francisco: Ignatius Press, 1989), 98.

[198] Jonathan Haidt, *The Anxious Generation: How the Great Rewiring of Childhood Is Causing an Epidemic of Mental Illness* (New York: Penguin Press, 2024), 27.

due to self-harm and suicide.[199] And these increases are affecting people of all faiths. Note that this is not an anxiety limited to what von Balthasar calls "secular" anxiety, which can and should be overcome by the Christian. Remember: At every Mass, we pray that we may be "safe from all distress"—from both secular anxiety and "sin anxiety."

This book is not so much about why anxiety rates are on the rise—many social scientists, psychologists, psychiatrists, neuroscientists, philosophers, and theologians have weighed in on this question.[200] Certainly, our increased use of social media has been shown to significantly ramp up anxiety and depression in young people, as Jonathan Haidt has carefully shown. There is also the general trend in our contemporary culture emphasizing achievement and production, even to the point of self-production and self-exploitation; this, too, is certainly a major contributing factor. However, this book is more of a practical one; we have written it for those of us who are struggling with anxiety, or who know someone struggling with it, and want to understand and take steps to remediate it.

---

[199] Ibid., 30–32.

[200] One compelling theory is presented by Jonathan Haidt in *The Anxious Generation: How the Great Rewiring of Childhood Is Causing an Epidemic of Mental Illness*, which argues, among other things, that the ever-increasing use of digital devices by children avoids the necessary interactive, embodied, and often risky play during which kids learned to develop social skills and to navigate the occasional fearful situation. Dr. Christopher Palmer presents another compelling theory in *Brain Energy*. Yet another, more philosophical, hypothesis is that of Byung-Chul Han, who pinpoints the contemporary focus on constant achievement and production that causes us to ceaselessly drive ourselves to achievement and even self-exploitation at the price of ever-increasing anxiety. As he puts it, the "neoliberal politics of production" require constant productivity fueled by anxiety.

We've discussed many ways anxiety manifests itself—whether through intrusive thoughts, dread, worry, ruminating for hours, sleeplessness, lack of energy, brain fog, chronic distractedness, cognitive distortions (for example, "I am worthless" or "I am unlovable"), helplessness, rage, scruples, or other debilitating emotions.

We've also discussed ways we try to manage anxiety, whether through more worrying, even meta-level worrying (i.e., worrying *about* worrying), numbing or distracting activities, avoiding the triggers, and so on. Ultimately, we discovered that one's "core defense" (or go-to attempted solution), whether intentional or not, is often an unhelpful strategy or defense—one that becomes an even greater problem than the original trigger for anxiety.

Good ways to handle anxiety include practicing mindfulness, reframing, and, most importantly, facing the anxiety itself. Facing the anxiety when we're experiencing it is often the best way to cue our amygdala (the threat center of our brain) that each particular trigger we encounter is not actually a threat. This process can be used not only with any trigger (for example, giving a speech, facing heights, intrusive thoughts, interpersonal conflict, etc.) but also with anxiety itself—thereby cueing our brains that we're not overcome by the threat of anxiety. Now we can face anxiety directly and even relish the opportunity to transform it into a means of personal growth.

Being able to confront anxiety and withstand it not only decreases the level of anxiety over time but also enables us to reframe it and say to ourselves, variously:

✢ "This anxiety I'm experiencing right now is adrenaline that will make me extra smart as I answer questions in my next interview!"

✢ "This anxiety (adrenaline) I'm experiencing right now will give me the energy and enthusiasm I need to meet new people at a party!"

✢ "This anxiety (adrenaline) I'm experiencing right now will help me give a truly motivating speech at Toastmasters!"

✢ "This anxiety (adrenaline) I'm experiencing right now will help me prepare well for the upcoming quiz."

✢ "This anxiety (adrenaline) I'm experiencing right now will help me run a faster 5K race!"

Anxiety need not be seen as a threat, but rather as an opportunity for growth.

Setting Up Our Children for Success

One of the key takeaways we'd like you to have as we wrap up this book is a point we emphasized back in chapter 5, which is that running from anxiety serves only to increase the anxiety. Our amygdala is always on the alert for avoidance behavior, and when we avoid something, our threat response increases.

Jonathan Haidt, social scientist and author of the bestselling book *The Anxious Generation*, claims that a major benefit of traditional childhood play, during which kids are on their own for many hours, learning to navigate various mishaps and to get along with diverse playmates and without the benefit of parental oversight, is that such play teaches resiliency. The resiliency and lack of fear that develop naturally as a result of facing fears are beneficial in the future; as children raised this way grow to adulthood, they experience less anxiety than their counterparts who were raised in a more "bubble-wrapped environment" when navigating new situations or social situations. Moreover, the exhilaration many young people experience when overcoming their fears leads to increased self-esteem and happiness.[201]

Art often tells a story from his own childhood about growing up in California and getting into mischief with his brothers. They used to sneak into an orange grove and help themselves to the oranges—but they didn't stop at just eating them. They would also hurl the oranges at each other until they exploded. They were finally caught in the act and chased down by the owner, who actually followed them all the way to their home, knocked on their door, and told their embarrassed parents that their kids were destroying his orange grove. Next time it happened, the farmer said, he'd be calling the police. Art recalls having to apologize to the farmer and promise never to trespass again.

[201] English journalist and writer Decca Aitkenhead wanted to test Haidt's theories, so she got her high-school-age kids and some of their friends to voluntarily give up their smartphones for four weeks and then go camping without adult supervision (they had "dumb" phones in case of emergency). The youth returned exhilarated and reported being happier than they had been in years. See her article in *The Sunday Times*, "What Happened When I Made My Sons and Their Friends Go without Smartphones," August 11, 2024, https://www.thetimes.com/life-style/parenting/article/what-happened-when-i-made-my-sons-and-their-friends-go-without-smartphones-vpcnbj58d.

Some of the lessons he and his brothers learned through that experience were the value of private property, the consequences of trespassing, and respect for another's hard work. They also learned the limits of their own freedom: that their freedom ought to be used for doing what is right and good — and not simply doing whatever they wanted. Art and his brothers learned that they cannot be indifferent to others while pursuing their own pleasure. The limits of their freedom must be modified by reality and by respect for others. Conflict that arises during play need not kill the ability to have fun; rather, it leads to growth instead of to a narcissistic self-reference and isolation. As Byung-Chul Han writes, "It is only from conflicts that stable relationships and identities ensue. A person grows and matures by working through conflict."[202]

We, as well as our children, discover in facing difficulties that we are more resilient than we thought, that the anxiety induced by the unknown is less fearsome than we suspected. Of course, we aren't suggesting that the degree of anxiety or fear we would allow children to face is the *same* as that to which an adult might experience. Nor would we, depending on the age and temperament of the child, expect them to face these situations alone: So often the loving presence of Mom or Dad is the *calming influence* needed to help children learn to regulate their own emotions. More importantly, parental love and guidance help children understand, manage, and handle many difficult — even potentially traumatic — experiences. We can acknowledge our children's fear and discomfort when facing a challenging situation, help them develop

---

[202] Byung-Chul Han, *The Expulsion of the Other* (Cambridge: Polity Press, 2018), 24.

coping skills, and encourage them to face the challenging situation: for example, "I know it can be awkward to sit with kids you don't know at lunch, but let's come up with some conversation starters." In short, taking age, temperament, and environment into consideration, we frequently don't realize that our children can often handle more than we allow them. The irony is that our age is one that wants to banish all negativity, all discomfort, all anxiety—yet never have we been more anxious. Psychiatrist Anna Lembke asked in *Dopamine Nation*: Is it possible that in our culture we have coddled and protected and praised and rewarded—"raising our children in the equivalent of a padded cell"—so much that our children cannot face even the slightest adversity or challenge, and, in fact, cannot even function in the world?[203] In wanting to eliminate all anxiety, we also eliminate the other. We make our entire world *smooth*, like an iPhone,[204] with no resistance to our own worldview, no negativity, no stranger. But who is more other than God? Eliminating all otherness ends up destroying our own humanity.

FACING DEATH: THE ULTIMATE CORE ANXIETY

"In our time, which strives to banish all negativity from life, death too falls silent.... It is no longer 'a way to be,' but rather no more than the mere end of life, which must be delayed by all means. Death simply means de-production, the end of

---

[203] Anna Lembke, *Dopamine Nation: Finding Balance in the Age of Indulgence* (New York: Dutton, 2021), 37.

[204] Byung-Chul Han, *Saving Beauty* (Cambridge: Polity Press, 2018), 1. "The smooth is the signature of the present time.... It embodies today's *society of positivity*."

production. Today, production has totalized itself to become the only way of life. The hysteria over health is ultimately the hysteria of production. Yet it destroys true vitality."[205]

In writing his book *A Time to Die*, journalist and author Nicolas Diat interviewed monks secluded in monasteries throughout Europe, including the silent Carthusians in the Grande Chartreuse. They are not afraid of death—which one might argue is the ultimate anxiety. In fact, they spend most of their lives meditating on eternity: "We must love this door that will allow us to know the Father. We are born for heaven."[206]

Cardinal Robert Sarah writes that our contemporary world is suffering from the "diabolical temptation" to do away with all finitude: weakness, fatigue, pain, sickness, and even death.[207] When we deny death as a part of life—as a preparation for and passageway to eternal life—as perhaps the final trial of life's journey toward eternal life and peace, we ignore the fact that it is now, during our earthy life, that we essentially *choose life or death* for ourselves (*CCC*, 1470). If we do not intentionally choose life—eternal life—we will choose death. This will be the ultimate death: essentially ignoring the "true" anxiety—anxiety based in a fear of death, a fear of potentially failing that final test, a fear of the unknown of our final reward. Rather than face this calmly and maturely, we are left with the anxiety that comes of living a lie, living in a way that ignores and even denies the fact

---

[205] Han, *Expulsion*, 29.

[206] Nicolas Diat, *A Time to Die: Monks on the Threshold of Eternal Life* (San Francisco: Ignatius Press, 2019), 166.

[207] Cardinal Robert Sarah, *The Day Is Now Far Spent* (San Francisco: Ignatius Press, 2019), 180.

that death waits for us all. What does this look like in practice? It is nothing more than a life of superficiality, distraction, and agitation, one in which we are constantly working, producing (even self-producing), all to keep ourselves from facing interior emptiness and fear. Cardinal Sarah writes convincingly that our affluent Western culture is experiencing the "radical, deliberately willed solitude of the damned."[208] We are, he says, like the rich young man of the Gospel (Mark 10:17–21), who turned away from happiness and the love of Christ because of his attachment to his many earthly possessions: "There you have the story of the West. It refused at the last moment to give everything. It balked at the supreme sacrifice. It was afraid, held back by its riches. So it sank into sadness."[209]

SURRENDERING TO CHRIST

Sometimes the riches we refuse to give up are our own plans or our dependence on our own abilities. We attempt to do everything relying on our own strength, as Bishop Conley discovered. We give lip service to the fact that we depend on God, but do we actually live as though we truly depend on Him? No; we behave as though we were in charge of it all, as though Jesus is merely our consultant, coach, or cheerleader on the sidelines. When this total self-reliance becomes really ingrained in our lives, we run the risk of breaking down, falling apart, and drowning in our own anxiety. Can we give up these possessions? Can we give up our will, our plans, our strength?

[208] Ibid., 123.
[209] Ibid., 124.

Thank God for giving us another way to live, an alternative path to that of nonstop achieving, striving, and anxiety. We must simply surrender to Him, let Him take the reins even as we abide in Him ever more deeply through prayer and the sacraments and intimate communion with Him. But there lies the rub — this giving over of ourselves is easier said than done: Can we truly surrender to God our life and death, our strength and weakness, and follow Our Lord Jesus Christ?

This is the message of the cross. We are told to take it up daily, not to avoid it at all cost. "And he said to all, 'If any man would come after me, let him deny himself and take up his cross daily and follow me'" (Luke 9:23). Daily taking up the opportunities to directly face our fears and anxieties is one way we can follow Jesus. And yet just as there is also joy in the cross, because Christ has transformed it, so, too, is there the possibility of joy in facing our anxieties. Jesus does not tell us that He wants us to be miserable and suffering through life. He tells us that He came so that we might have life and have it abundantly (John 10:10). He doesn't ask us to take up only that part of the cross that is scourging, humiliation, and death — though He may ask us to suffer in these ways. But remember what St. Rose of Lima is credited with saying: Grace increases as the struggle increases. If He asks us to suffer great hardships, He will also supply the grace, the joy, and the love to bear them as we ought.

As Catholic spiritual writer Caryll Houselander notes so beautifully:

> We should not forget that Christ did not bring
> the suffering of his Passion to us; he brought his

infinite love to us, it is we who gave the suffering to him. He gives suffering the power of his love, and therefore when we accept the suffering necessarily involved in living the Christ-life in this world, we are not submerging ourselves more deeply into suffering than we need have done, but are doing something which will transform it ultimately into joy.... The Christ-life is a joyful one, but it is hard, it is not easy, because it is never for one moment the line of least resistance; it is a continual conquest.[210]

"If then the light in you is darkness, how great is the darkness!" (Matt. 6:23). The light is the lamp of the soul radiating the light of Christ within us, the flame that burns ever brighter the closer our souls are to the beloved. With the oil of grace, of virtue, of prayer, it will burn more brightly. But what if our souls are not fed with the oil?

BLINDED BY OUR DISTRACTIONS

Surprising though it may be, when we never enter into the interior castle of our souls, we're like those poor souls St. Teresa of Ávila describes in the *Interior Castle* who spend all their time outside of *their own castle*, roaming around in the darkness with snakes, reptiles, and the evil creatures of the night. For a more immediate application of this image, it's like when we're on the Internet, gazing through the windowless Windows,[211]

---

[210] *Magnificat* 26, no. 4 (2024): 143.
[211] Han, *Expulsion*, 47: "Windows is a window with no view."

grasping and consuming, doomscrolling, and filled with anxiety. How great will the darkness be! St. Teresa writes, "It seems as though they are incapable of entering within themselves at all. So accustomed have they grown to living all the time with the reptiles and other creatures to be found in the outer court of the castle that they have almost become like them; and although by nature they are so richly endowed as to having the power of holding converse with none other than God Himself, there is nothing that can be done for them."[212]

When we spend our days entirely on the surface, caught up in a state of problem-solving and "productivity," of hyperactivity and distractions—in short, when we do not take the time to retreat in silence into our "inner room" to pray to God and to meditate on His Word—we face instead a constant, ever-present daily anxiety: "Today's anxiety ... takes place within the everyday consensus. It is an everyday fear. Its subject remains the 'they': 'The ego orients itself by the others and spins out of control when it no longer believes it can keep up.... The thought of what the others think of oneself, and what they think that others think of them, thus becomes a source of social anxiety. It is not the objective situation that burdens and breaks the individual so much as the feeling of drawing the short straw compared to significant others.'"[213]

And really, not even to significant others. Somehow we now feel pressured to live up to simply any *similar* other that we come across on social media.

[212] Teresa of Ávila, *Interior Castle*, trans. and ed. E. Allison Peers (New York: Image Books, 1989), 31.

[213] Han, *Expulsion*, 32. Han is here quoting Heinz Dude, *Gesellschaft der Angst.*

Turning toward God's Grace and Presence

When we pray at every Mass that "we may be always free from sin and safe from all distress," we're not asking God to grant us a trouble-free life, for Christ has already told us that in this life, there will be trouble (John 16:33). Rather, we're asking to be free from *sin*—not difficulties and trouble—and safe from distress. Our safety is in Him, as Bishop Conley took to heart. In Him, we will have peace. But not peace as the world gives it: "Peace I leave with you; my peace I give to you; not as the world gives do I give to you. Let not your hearts be troubled, neither let them be afraid" (John 14:27). We are seeking interior peace, the peace of Christ that keeps our hearts calm with trust and confidence in God.

Mindfulness, reframing, and leaning into anxiety are steps we take on the natural level. With the help of God's grace, we can achieve and maintain interior peace through the cultivation of a life of prayer, growth in virtue, and frequent reception of the sacraments. And the fruit of our prayer, as Scripture tells us, should be love, joy, peace, patience, kindness, goodness, faithfulness, gentleness, and self-control (Gal 5:22–23).

Without the virtues of temperance and fortitude, we will find it much more tempting to take the easy route, to go with the knee-jerk reaction or the quick fix—in other words, the wide road that leads to destruction. But in fact, fighting the good fight to foster these virtues will help us to attain true freedom—not the "freedom to create ourselves" that will ultimately drive us to anxiety and despair. True freedom is the freedom to do what is right, to do God's will because He alone knows what is best for our souls and wills for us that ultimate happiness found with Him in Heaven. But make no mistake: There is no resurrection without the cross. The way to glory passes through the way of the cross.

How can we face this way of the cross without that great virtue of fortitude that gives us a firm disposition to overcome our fears for the sake of a true ideal, a noble end? In the heat of an argument, when emotions are running high, what constrains us from hurling at our loved one ugly words of reproach? It is fortitude, namely, the strength to hold our tongues when tempted to explode in angry words—the strength to die to ourselves for the sake of our marriage or our relationships. And it is temperance that keeps us from letting our runaway emotions take charge; it is how we restrain ourselves, how we refrain from hurling angry, hurtful, or contemptuous words, all for the sake of the other. As St. Paul cautions us, "You were called to freedom, brethren; only do not use your freedom as an opportunity for the flesh, but through love be servants of one another" (Gal. 5:13).

A Calm Deliverance from the Furnace of Anxiety

Anticipating discoveries that would be made centuries later by neuroscientists, St. Francis de Sales emphasized that anxiety is only increased by the attempt to deliver oneself of "every pressing evil." Instead of attempting this, he advises that we patiently and calmly accept all trials out of love for God. And in fact, as he reminded us in chapter 9, when we're struggling and fluttering like birds caught in a net, we wind up only furthering the hold that anxiety has on us. The key is to keep our "souls in our hand," as de Sales advised, and to "look to God's Goodness and Providence":

> If any one strives to be delivered from his troubles out of love of God, he will strive patiently, gently, humbly and calmly, looking for deliverance rather to God's Goodness and Providence than to his own industry or efforts; but if self-love is the prevailing object he will grow hot and eager in seeking relief, as though all depended more upon himself than upon God. I do not say that the person thinks so, but he acts eagerly as though he did think it. Then if he does not find what he wants at once, he becomes exceedingly impatient and troubled, which does not mend matters, but on the contrary makes them worse, and so he gets into an unreasonable state of anxiety and distress, till he begins to fancy that there is no cure for his trouble. Thus you see how a disturbance, which was right at the outset, begets anxiety, and anxiety goes on into an excessive distress, which is exceedingly dangerous.[214]

Through it all, we stay resolute in facing the cross of anxiety. Even when our boat is pummeled by waves and buffeted by the raging wind, we strive to remain calm in our innermost

---

[214] Francis de Sales, *Introduction to the Devout Life* (London: Rivington, 1876; Veritatis Splendor Publications, 2012), 198ff.

being. We keep our eyes on the lodestar of our love for Christ, of God's loving kindness, and of His Providence. We firmly believe that God's grace is with us, now, in each present moment, even though we may not feel His presence. As St. Francis de Sales wrote to a friend who was suffering from fear, "Be firm in your resolutions. Stay in the boat. Let the storm come. While Jesus lives, you will not die."[215]

[215] Christopher Blum and Joshua Hochschild, *A Mind at Peace: Reclaiming an Ordered Soul in the Age of Distraction* (Manchester, NH: Sophia Institute Press, 2017), 32.

About the Authors

Art Bennett is a licensed marriage and family therapist with more than thirty-five years' experience in the field. He co-founded the Alpha-Omega clinics in Virginia and Maryland, which integrated mental health with the Catholic Faith, and he worked for ten years as president and CEO of Catholic Charities in the Diocese of Arlington. He currently practices at Bennett Therapy and Consulting in Northern Virginia. He has coauthored with his wife, Laraine, five books: *The Temperament God Gave You*, *The Temperament God Gave Your Spouse*, *The Temperament God Gave Your Kids*, *The Emotions God Gave You*, and *Tuned In: The Power of Pressing Pause and Listening*.

Laraine Bennett holds a master of arts in philosophy and is the author of *The Little Way of Living with Less: Learning to Let Go with the Little Flower* and *A Year of Grace: 365 Reflections for Caregivers*. She created the game *KNOW THYSELF: The Game of Temperaments*.

The Bennetts reside in Northern Virginia and have four adult children, including Dr. Lianna Bennett Haidar, and eleven grandchildren.

Dr. Lianna Bennett Haidar is a clinical psychologist who works with clients to heal past traumas, reduce the experiences of depression and anxiety, and improve the quality of their relationships. As a Catholic therapist, Dr. Haidar utilizes a variety of treatment approaches, particularly those focused on healing trauma with the integration of faith and psychology. Dr. Haidar has a private practice, Bennett Psychotherapy, PLLC. She lives in Northern Virginia with her husband and two children.

Sophia Institute

Sophia Institute is a nonprofit institution that seeks to nurture the spiritual, moral, and cultural life of souls and to spread the gospel of Christ in conformity with the authentic teachings of the Roman Catholic Church.

Sophia Institute Press fulfills this mission by offering translations, reprints, and new publications that afford readers a rich source of the enduring wisdom of mankind.

Sophia Institute also operates the popular online resource CatholicExchange.com. *Catholic Exchange* provides world news from a Catholic perspective as well as daily devotionals and articles that will help readers to grow in holiness and live a life consistent with the teachings of the Church.

In 2013, Sophia Institute launched Sophia Institute for Teachers to renew and rebuild Catholic culture through service to Catholic education. With the goal of nurturing the spiritual, moral, and cultural life of souls, and an abiding respect for the role and work of teachers, we strive to provide materials and programs that are at once enlightening to the mind and ennobling to the heart; faithful and complete, as well as useful and practical.

Sophia Institute gratefully recognizes the Solidarity Association for preserving and encouraging the growth of our apostolate over the course of many years. Without their generous and timely support, this book would not be in your hands.

www.SophiaInstitute.com
www.CatholicExchange.com
www.SophiaTeachers.org

Sophia Institute Press is a registered trademark of Sophia Institute.
Sophia Institute is a tax-exempt institution as defined by the
Internal Revenue Code, Section 501(c)(3). Tax ID 22-2548708.